LOOKING FOR

LYRICS

WOW!

Strings Of The Heart

Edited by Vivien Linton

First published in Great Britain in 2010 by:

 Young**Writers**

Young Writers
Remus House
Coltsfoot Drive
Peterborough
PE2 9JX
Telephone: 01733 890066
Website: www.youngwriters.co.uk

Foreword

Young Writers was established in 1991 to nurture creativity in our children and young adults, to give them an interest in poetry and an outlet to express themselves. Seeing their work in print will encourage them to keep writing as they grow, and become our poets of tomorrow.

Selecting the poems has been challenging and immensely rewarding. The effort and imagination invested by these young writers makes their poems a pleasure to enjoy reading time and time again.

Contents

The Poems

You And Me

Verse 1
You're so strong when I am gone,
There's no one else on my side.
When you're here you light the room
But now I'm left in the dark.
Can't you see I need you?
Can't you see I want you in my heart?

Chorus
Now you're gone,
You've left me here just a second ago.
I'm so sad, but you're so glad,
I've needed you from the start . . .

Verse 2
Can you remember when we first met?
Can you remember all that laughter?
Can't you see
Can't you see you're the one for me?

Chorus
Now you're gone,
You've left me here just a second ago.
I'm so sad, but you're so glad,
I've needed you from the start . . .

Verse 3
If I had another life,
I would spend it all with you.
If there was another path,
I would go along with you.
But if you're not here with me,
Life will not be.

Chorus
Now you're gone,
You've left me here just a second ago.
I'm so sad, but you're so glad,
I've needed you from the start.

Georgia Ody (11)

Don't Stop For The Music

La, la, la, la, la, la, la, la, la, la, la, la,
La, la, la, la, la, la, la, la.

Don't stop, don't stop, don't stop for the music, rock
Let's just do this!

Chorus
Don't stop for the music, rock,
Let's just do this, rock,
Let's just do this, rock, la, la.
Don't stop for the music, hot,
Let's just groove it, hot,
Let's just groove it, hot, la, la.
I dropped champagne on the floor,
Won't you gimme some more?
Won't you gimme some more, some more, more?

Don't stop. Woah, woah. Just rock.
With beat in the air in the street in a fair
With the beat woah, woah, woah.
I feel alive when I'm playing this song.
I don't care if I sing it wrong, woah, woah, woah, woah.
I feel alive. I feel alive. I feel alive.
That's why I'm singing this song.

Chorus
Don't stop for the music, rock,
Let's just do this, rock,
Let's just do this, rock, la, la.
Don't stop for the music, hot,
Let's just groove it, hot,
Let's just groove it, hot, la, la.
I dropped champagne on the floor,
Won't you gimme some more?
Won't you gimme some more, some more, more?

Every time I go to a party it's boring.
I just want the disco lights to shine on me.
But there's always someone else who gets the glee.
They're always dancing with the beat
And I'm always stood cos it's too hard to see.

La, la, la, la, la, la, la,
I feel alive.

Chorus
Don't stop for the music, rock,
Let's just do this, rock,
Let's just do this, rock, la, la.
Don't stop for the music, hot,
Let's just groove it, hot,
Let's just groove it, hot, la, la.
I dropped champagne on the floor,
Won't you gimme some more?
Won't you gimme some more, some more, more?

With night partying around
But with the glass light jumping round
With the moon and the night we don't make a sound
But to repeat this loud
If I feel alive with the party tonight
And the music round and the kids at the bottom
They don't make a sound, no woah, no woah.

Everything's spinning and I'm kind of going dizzy,
Cos the girl in front is very frizzy
And I carry on dancing but something kinda strange happened
I woke up in my bed the very next day
Yeah, oh la, la, la, la, la, ooh.

Chorus
Don't stop for the music, rock,
Let's just do this, rock,
Let's just do this, rock, la, la.
Don't stop for the music, hot,
Let's just groove it, hot,
Let's just groove it, hot, la, la.
I dropped champagne on the floor,
Won't you gimme some more?
Won't you gimme some more, some more, more?

I love to party, woah.
I love to party, woah (x 3)

Eleanor Smith (12)

Appreciating Diversity

You're walking down the street,
And you see a guy in a hoody,
You don't want to meet
Cos all the while you're thinking
Would he? Thinking, *has he got a knife,*
A bomb, or a gun?
Is he gonna kill me, just for a laugh
And some fun?
He starts walking faster; it's nearly a run,
Reaches his hand into his pocket.
You're thinking, *he's getting his gun!*
He's nearly level with you
And you start to scream,
Till you realise that it's not what it seems.
The guy takes his hood down
And reaches out his hand
To a homeless man on the street,
Just sitting on bare land,
Hands him over some money
And sends over a warm smile,
Tries to be quite funny,
Tries to keep his style.
Putting his hood back on,
He begins to walk on by,
You feel ashamed, you ask yourself *why?*
Why did I think that? Why did I judge?
Why did I foolishly form a grudge
Against a stranger who I've never met?
Form these opinions thinking,
I bet, I bet he's got a gun,
I bet he's got a knife,
I bet he's got a son but not got a wife,
I bet he skives school to deal and make drugs,
Thinking he's so cool, hanging round with thugs.
But then you finally realise
What you're doing wrong
And think back to that meaningful song,
Everyone's the same, no matter their fame,
Playing the same game,

4

On this planet, we all came,
To live our life, to be ourselves,
To be treated equal, poor or wealth,
No one deserves this prejudice hate,
So take a step back and try to create
A world, a society, a city, a town,
A school, a college, all around,
Where none of this unjust hatred exists.
People learn to civilise, without blood or fists,
A place where you can trust to be yourself
Without being judged on appearance or wealth.
A place where you can trust other people,
Without being scared of falling deeper.
There's more to me than what you see,
So let me be myself, let me run free,
It's that easy, thankfully
To appreciate the fact that you and me
Are actually quite similar,
Even though we're different
And this I prefer, is what I've learnt,
To appreciate similarities and also differences,
To seize the opportunity
And it's not just a coincidence,
That I know you're thinking that this is quite true,
So next time you see a hoody and all his crew,
Don't judge before you know what he's going through,
'Cause soon, but hopefully not,
That homeless guy might be you . . .
There's more to me than what you see
And the same goes for you, I'm sure you'll agree.

Hafsah Ali (15)

World's Greatest Show

I'm watching the show, and I know
That it will end one day or another
I'll drive further to achieve the prize,
but there's bad news, the sunshine's in my eyes
But I'll get there, because life will share a little bit of goodness and badness
Life will bounce you off the walls, it's just madness
The more I drive, the more I'll dive into the roller coaster,
it's gonna be fun
What happens when it's done?

Chorus
I'm driving all night long, listening to my favourite song
I'll get there one day, maybe not this day
but I know I'm strong
The more life challenges me
the more I see, what the world's got for me,
It's the world's greatest show
I'll learn more each day, maybe with nothing to say
But I'll still learn, which means I'll earn more knowledge about this life.
The guests arrive, the show begins
life's just a show in front of your eyes with hellos and goodbyes
Watch the water, daddy's daughter isn't a kid anymore,
There's gonna be a day where I'll go out that door,
the more he's terrible
The more he isn't frightable
so let's just leave it at that ... because

Chorus
I'm driving all night long, listening to my favourite song.
I'll get there one day, maybe not this day,
but I know I'm strong
The more life challenges me
the more I see, what the world's got for me.
It's the world's greatest show
The night has fallen, let's get this rolling
so we might break tonight
But we'll still fight, let's just drive
so we can dive into this life-like roller coaster ... because
I'm driving all night long, listening to my favourite song.
I'll get there one day, maybe not this day,

but I know I'm strong
The more life challenges me, the more I see what the world's got for me,
Daddy's little girl isn't so small,
she'll break down your walls
And fight back ... Because

Chorus
I'm driving all night long, listening to my favourite song.
I'll get there one day, maybe not this day,
but I know I'm strong
The more life challenges me, the more I see what the world's got for me,
it's the world's greatest show.
Life is war, easy or hard
Prince Charming with his shiny sword
slay the dragon
I'm wearing my mother's cardigan, she made for me,
because she loves me and she's preparing me for ...
I'm driving all night long, listening to my favourite song.
I'll get there one day, maybe not this day,
but I know I'm strong
the more life challenges me, the more I see, what the world's got for me,
Oh, oh, woah ... I'll get there one day, maybe not today!
Because woah,
It's the world's greatest show!

Eileidh Greig (13)

The Fight

You come, right here, right now
You're probably scared wondering how
The bell's just gone
The fight is now officially on
Right jab, left jab, uppercut, you're down
I gotta feeling you're leaving town
When we go back to school
It will be sooooo cool
I think it's fair
Come back if you dare.

Wasim Hussain (12)

Daisy Chains

My childhood memories
Take me back to tree climbing days
My hand in yours on the very top branch
I knew that if I fell
You'd always be there to catch me
For sure

Only seven years old
But we knew love
Love at its most pure
All the girls in your class at school
Do they love you like I do?

Hours upon hours we'd play in your garden
Laughing as we raced to the conservatory door
Our parents dining on the porch
Plastic chairs scraping on the patio floor
Friends since their own childhoods
So many of their memories
We'd yet to endure

We knew one day we'd walk down the aisle
You and me
Friends for evermore
You'd propose a million times
With a ring made of daisy chains

Summer days when our families camped
In your grandmother's field
Riding your mum's old horse
Sitting one behind the other on his dusty back
In the paddock of green clover

Then the holidays were over
And we returned home
It seemed like a million miles away from you
From us
From forever until the next

So many years passed us by
When the camping trips became
So much less frequent

Until the day on your 18th birthday
A year before my own

One look in your eyes
And our childhood sparkled before me
My heart squeezed at the sight of your long-gone yet familiar face
Your girlfriend? So what?
Why does anything matter today
When we finally have each other again?

Ten more years
Down the line
And our childish fantasy
Is finally coming true
My white dress
Your smart suit
And the words
That bind us forever
And the golden ring
That you slip on my finger
Has daisy chains
Engraved around the edge.

Caitlin Ford (12)

My Grandad's Grave

Standing silently by the gate
Looking at a field of white stones,
I look down at the bunch of flowers I am holding
- to put -
Where a loved one once stood.

I can feel the tears tumbling down my cheeks
And into my dry mouth,
I stumble around,
That is when I see the grave,
I fall to my knees and place the flowers,
By the headstone.

Even though I did not know him, I want him back.

Lucy Whitear (13)

Break Away

Verse 1
There are heavens above us, in the sky.
The angels cometh, but they don't know why.
They've descended to find the truth.
There's more good than evil, where's the proof.
Before I fall, I say to you all, this is my last call.
I'm singing songs in my head,
I've put my thoughts to bed,
I can't help but be filled with dread.

Chorus
Don't defy me, don't even try me.
I know that I will cry, when this feeling dies.
I think you'll find this the end of the line.
You had better hide, or I will find . . . you.
I am outta my mind, trying to deal with your kind.
It's time to break away, cos time will fade,
And it seems all the good days . . .
They have been played.

Verse 2
I'm feeling confusion, over you.
I've lost another, no that can't be true.
We've just started, but we're all run down.
I try my hardest, but there's no crown.
The months have rolled by,
Like tears run down your face.
I can no longer protect you in this place.
I want someone to find me and set me free,
But I'm blinded by hate, I can no longer see!

Chorus
Don't defy me, don't even try me.
I know that I will cry, when this feeling dies.
I think you'll find this the end of the line.
You had better hide, or I will find . . . you.
I am outta my mind, trying to deal with your kind.
It's time to break away, cos time will fade,
And it seems all the good days . . .
They have been played.

Chorus
Don't defy me, don't even try me.
I know that I will cry, when this feeling dies.
I think you'll find this the end of the line.
You had better hide, or I will find . . . you.
I am outta my mind, trying to deal with your kind.
It's time to break away, cos time will fade,
And it seems all the good days . . .
They have been played.

Verse 3
This is my ecstasy, this is who I should be,
The clouds roll over me, reflected in the sea.
I don't mind being by myself.
At least that way I'm not on the shelf.
Down this road I shall go, never gonna stop,
Never gonna slow.
This is for the best, just let me say,
The further I walk, the further we break away.

Mathew Hoare (14)

We Are Human

Our eyes are like dead stars,
burning in circles, we're living
but we're empty inside.
We are blind of the beauty, sightful of the cold.
Emotionless, uncaring without love or lust
all that we have left is hate
and if we cry we will rust.
They watch us for entertainment
we are all stars in a TV show called Life.
Their useless cosmetics
make us feel old,
I know now that all that
really glitters is cold,
as cold as our metallic hearts.
We are human.

Eliot Lingwood (12)

Ghost Beach

They are around me, surrounding me
Everywhere I look I see the faces of the innocent
Why did they have to go? Why?
It's not fair, but life really isn't fair anyway
They are shouting, I am shouting, but there is nothing I can do

Chorus
It will never be the same without them,
Please, let them rest in paradise
I don't want to do this anymore,
Walking down the sand
Watch out, don't go in the zone,
I am in the zone, the Ghost Beach zone
I said watch out, don't go in the zone,
I am in the zone, the Ghost Beach zone

What's this? I can see a baby boy, this isn't fair!
I'm reaching out, telling him to hold my hand
I feel like I'm running out of time, but there is nothing I can do
Straight from my heart I know that there is no chance . . .
The temperature is ice cold, compared with this the Antarctic is nothing
There seems to be a deadly connection, ghostly
I look straight up to the heavens,
Asking for them to return back home here
I wish I could change the game, but it's no use, I have lost

Chorus
It will never be the same without them,
Please, let them rest in paradise
I don't want to do this anymore,
Walking down the sand
Watch out, don't go in the zone,
I am in the zone, the Ghost Beach zone
I said watch out, don't go in the zone,
I am in the zone, the Ghost Beach zone

I am serious, please help me, stranded on the Ghost Beach
They are speaking, drawing me into them
They want me to join them, join them in the realm of light and darkness
I now need to make a choice
No. Time's up. Decision has been made

Chorus
It will never be the same without them,
Please, let them rest in paradise
I don't want to do this anymore,
Walking down the sand
Watch out, don't go in the zone,
I am in the zone, the Ghost Beach zone
I said watch out, don't go in the zone,
I am in the zone, the Ghost Beach zone.

Phillip Rosser (16)

Out There

When I walk into the street,
With everything just at my feet,
And I wonder what it's like,
To rule the world.

As I'm sitting by myself,
And I'm thinking of the things that I want to do,
It suddenly feels like I'm on to something new,
Something deeper than what I am right now.

Deeper and deeper,
That's where I'm gonna stay,
Closer and closer,
To the truth why you went away.

I'm wondering if,
There's a life out there,
Just waiting,
For me to come around.

But with my head in the clouds,
And my heart still on the ground,
I know that there is something,
To find out there,
Right here,
To find,
Out there.

Chantal Elian (13)

A Footballer's Dream

All I have wanted from my life is to help my country
Win the World Cup
And for me to score the winning goal.
To be a part of the winning team
Would be the best thing to happen to me
And Scotland's A team,
Winning would be great.
Singing my name after a goal at 89 minutes
Would be the pleasure I have been dreaming of
All my life.
England's goalkeeper to let in a belter of a goal
Would put a cherry on top of my night.
Wouldn't it be fabulous to win, win, win?
For me it would definitely be the greatest thing.

A yellow, then a red card wasn't expected;
Arguing with the ref wasn't a big surprise.
Only one fight during the match,
Could there be another when the tension increases?
A penalty kick because of foul play,
Goalie on his toes, what a great goal!
Studs to the face, elbows to the ribs,
How can the ref not notice this disgrace?

Wouldn't it be fabulous to win, win, win?
For me it would definitely be the greatest thing.
The half-time whistle goes and the fans rush
To get a hot pie or a bridie.
A Bovril, coffee, tea or Coke,
Depending on the good old Scottish weather.
Waiting in the queue takes some amount of time,
Hungry football fans push and shout.
When the whistle goes for the second half,
Groans from angry fans who haven't received their many snacks.

Wouldn't it be fabulous to win, win, win?
For me it would definitely be the greatest thing.
Leaving the stadium after a win is the hardest thing to do,
Hopefully the group calms down.
Scotland's fans are jumping with joy after a win.

England's fans hang their heads in a pit of despair.
The streets echo from the singing and chants,
Drivers getting angry with the happy fans on the road.
Everyone in Scotland has a smile on their face,
Everyone in England has a frown on their face.

Wouldn't it be fabulous to win, win, win?
For me it would definitely be the greatest thing.

Lindsay Crawford (13)

In Love

I watched out the window,
As the blue sky turned black.
It reminds me of your eyes,
Dark with stars in.
But that's just the problem,
You're taking over my mind.
'Cause when I close my eyes, you're there, smiling at me
And when I open my eyes, I wish it could be.

Chorus
Because I'm lying on a rain cloud in the middle of a desert,
And I'm walking on water every day.
I'm never gonna give up,
I just don't know what to do.
Because I'm head over heels,
In love with you.

Your face is like a picture in my head,
Your voice is like a tape recorder on repeat.
I need you here, I need you here with me.

Chorus
Because I'm lying on a rain cloud in the middle of a desert,
And I'm walking on water every day.
I'm never gonna give up,
I just don't know what to do.
Because I'm head over heels,
In love with you.

Jayne Hardy (14)

Familiars

In the darkness
They send chills down my spine
The bare, descending moon
Has burst into life
Hunting and suffering with prisoned eyes,
Familiars play in moonlit skies.

Beautiful wings the servants possess
With claws so sharp they can only be from the depths
Beautiful wings the servants possess
With claws so sharp they can only be from the . . .

This ordinary world ain't set in stone as I thought it'd be,
Just like haunted prey,
Familiars are haunting me
Familiars . . .

The nerves from the creatures that you receive
Black magic is here,
Bow down to its knees
No emotion, familiars can scream
The adrenaline rush takes over so fast.

Beautiful wings the servants possess,
With claws so sharp they can only be from the depths.
Beautiful wings the servants possess,
With claws so sharp they can only be from the . . .

This ordinary world ain't set in stone as I thought it'd be,
Just like haunted prey,
Familiars are haunting me
Familiars . . .

These blue hearts,
They will scream,
They will scream,
They will scream,
You feel them screaming, mourning in the shadows,
They will scream.
Scream,
Familiars . . .

This ordinary world ain't set in stone as I thought it'd be,
Just like haunted prey,
Familiars are haunting me
Familiars are haunting me,
They're haunting me
They're haunting me,
Familiars are haunting me
Familiars . . .

Charlotte Riley (17)

Not Asking For A Miracle

I guess I've been through some tough times in my life
I've yet to work out if it's worth the strife
I know it's there to strengthen me
But when I fall I can hardly see.

I'm not asking for a miracle
Just for you to hold me still
I need you to be there
Hold my hand
Show your love and care
And to understand.

Please wake me from this dream
Tell me everything's alright, they're not as they seem
Walk with me all the way, never stray
And say I'm nearing the end of the storm.

I can't believe all I've faced
It's been so confusing
It's like I've been aced
Tell me I haven't been fooled
But we're all slaves to this common game.

I'm not asking for a miracle
Just hold me tight and hold me still
I need you to be there
Hold my hand
Show your love and care
And to understand.

Chantelle Greenman (14)

Reunited

I got up one morning and signed into Facebook
A bunch of updates awaiting a glance or a look
Some photos uploaded by a family member
And her face lighting up one of them I remember.

I thought of the day when she passed away
And all the sadness it caused
And all the hearts broken.

But Heaven is the place to be
No more pain or suffering
Now you're watching over all of us
Immortal life and peace at mind
No one will be left behind
When loved ones are reunited.

Then comes the day when the other half of a heart
Enters those gates, joins the angels and from us he parts
But the hope that he is greeted by his saving grace
Eases the hurt, makes time pass by at a faster pace.

Then the deja-vu sets in with you
And this madness reignites
And it breaks us slowly.

But Heaven is the place to be
No more pain or suffering
Now you're watching over all of us
Immortal life and peace at mind
No one will be left behind
When loved ones are reunited.

But I want you close - right by my side
With all my heart, I need strength inside
Please, I miss you.

But Heaven is the place to be
No more pain or suffering
Now you're watching over all of us
Immortal life and peace at mind
No one will be left behind
When loved ones are reunited.

At long last that day has come
We return to where we're from
And all the past is locked away.
Now my dream's come true
We are all now with you
We have finally become, reunited.

India Oldfield-Cherry (14)

Funny Weather

Funny weather
My umbrella won't see through this storm
It's an outbreak of salvation
Waterfalls of liqueur may be the cure.

Chorus
Broken glass
Smashed windowpanes
The jigsaws broke now who's to blame
No super glue, we've all run out
My heart is broken without a doubt
Yeah, my heart is broken without a doubt.

Oh, this funny weather
Heavy greyness and pain
Claps of sound as doors slam
But a little girl does what she can.

Chorus
Funny weather
Rain disperses the past
The clouds they have changed
Unknowingly it's the beginning
Not the last.

Chorus
Funny weather
My umbrella won't see through this storm
It's an outbreak of salvation
Waterfalls of liquor may be the cure.

Alysha Woolley (15)

There Will Always Be Love

I'm special, I'm different
I'm not ready for a horrific event
My love will be true
And there is nothing you can do
My love is love and it will always be love

    Love was once my friend
    I thought love could never end
    But then it hit me
    That there was never a time we would agree
    We were in love, in love with Cupid
    Although it may seen stupid
    Cupid was the one with the arrows.
    All those arrows
    Cupid was our little friend
    Until he met his end
    Now everyone breaks up
    In the saddest way
    But not me
    Not me

I'm special, I'm different
I'm not ready for a horrific event
My love will be true
And there's nothing you can do
My love is love it will always be love

    There are always arguments
    Though love is such a present
    But then why all this hatred?
    Love is almost dead
    But we bring it back
    When there is no one else to attack
    Cupid was our little friend
    Until he met his end
    Now everyone breaks up
    In the saddest way.

I'm special, I'm different
I'm not ready for a horrific event
My love will be true
And there's nothing you can do
My love is love and it will always be love.

Rebecca Wood (13)

Mistake

Oops I did it again
I broke your heart like I did before
Please baby don't walk out on me
I promise I will love you as much as you love me
I love you
I love you
Baby I love you.

I made a mistake
That I should have never done
I made a mistake
That hurt everyone
I made a mistake
But I still love you.

Oops I hurt you again
I left you alone when you needed me the most
I know I hurt you but don't forget
All the memories and the great times we had
But most of all I will always love you.

I made a mistake
That I should have never done
I made a mistake
That hurt everyone
I made a mistake
But I still love you
I love you
I love you
Baby I love you.

Beth Taylor (12)

A Land Without Law

My happy days are dead and gone
The good in life is just a con
Precious metals, silver, gold,
The sun froze up, the world gone cold.
I hate to say, I'm on my own,
I have a shotgun, not a phone.
The human race, they are all gone,
Don't worry about me, I'll get along.
They say that war would help us all.
I told them, 'Don't be a fool!'
I was right, they were wrong
I'll cry no more, I will be strong!
I hate to say, I'm on my own,
I have a shotgun, not a phone.
The human race, they are all gone,
Don't worry about me, I'll get along.
I've been through Hell about 20 times
It gets harder the more I try.
I thought my friends were always there
But now I feel I could not care.
I hate to say, I'm on my own,
I have a shotgun, not a phone.
The human race, they are all gone,
Don't worry about me, I'll get along.
Rest in peace, the human race.
You all died at a fast pace.
Lightning, thunder across the sky,
Hitting the ground in the blink of an eye.
I hate to say, I'm on my own,
I have a shotgun, not a phone.
The human race, they are all gone,
Don't worry about me, I'll get along.
I'm the last one left, it's my chance now.
There's evil afoot, I sense it, how?
I've gotta pull this world out of the dark,
I'm fed up with this evil lark.
I hate to say, I'm on my own,
I have a shotgun, not a phone.
The human race, they are all gone,

Don't worry about me, I'll get along.
I hate to say, I'm on my own,
I have a shotgun, not a phone.
The human race, they are all gone,
Don't worry about me, I'll get along.

Joshua Bernard-Cooper (10)

Tears I Cry

When I'm alone,
I look in the past,
I look deep inside,
And hide away,
So you don't see
The tears I cry.

I used to stand up tall,
Be bold and brave,
Not anymore, I've changed,
I can't breathe,
I can't talk,
I despise myself,
Because of the tears I cry.

I don't cry on the outside,
It's the weakness in my eyes,
I don't have the answer,
So I walk away,
I'm torn to pieces
For those tears I cry.

I used to help the others,
Be strong and firm,
Not anymore, I've changed,
I can't sing,
I can't dance,
Right now all I think about
Are the tears I cry,
I'm the one to blame.

Mariah Hussain (13)

Who Am I?

Verse 1
Have you ever looked up to the sky
And wondered why?
Why are we here, what are we doing?
Spending every day with the worry
That you'll do something wrong
Or have to say sorry

Chorus
Ohhh
What is life?
How does it all work out?
What do we do, how do we do it?
We are wasting our lives, wasting our lives
Trying to figure out the truth

Verse 2
Have you ever wondered why we're here
With the fear of finding out who you are inside
Eating us alive
Watching the world go by
Trying to survive

Chorus
Ohhh
What is life?
How does it all work out?
What do we do, how do we do it?
We are wasting our lives, wasting our lives
Trying to figure out the truth

Verse 3
I'm so confused
Somebody give me some answers please
Can anybody hear me?
I'm begging on my knees
    (Repeat)

Chorus
Ohhh
What is life?

How does it all work out?
What do we do, how do we do it?
We are wasting our lives, wasting our lives
Wasting our lives, wasting our lives
(Go quieter, end with whisper).

Laura Hatherly (14)

Stop I Want To Get Off

Pop a pill, smoke a joint, drink a drink,
Be sick in a sink! Every day just seems the same
Pop a pill ease the pain!
When I'm up and when I'm down
We will face up to life with a frown
But is the pain worth losing your life?
Why don't you just get out of bed and fight!

Today I woke up, you weren't there and for a long time
I didn't care, I hadn't met anyone new!
But we had come and we had flew
In the cold light of day
All the old fears had gone away
Return I know they might; but I won't let them back
Without a fight!
I must move on and start afresh
For once breathe the smell of my own success
So time goes by as we know the pain may even seem to go

Is there anything I can say to you or change
Your life in an afternoon?
Or take away your pain for a while
Hold your hand or even just smile?
I have no money or riches to give
But a helping hand and a bit of a lift
Joy and peace and understanding
So please, just take my hand!

Stop I want to get off.
Never-ending circle of life!

Megan Sherlock (15)

Cast Off From My Door

I never thought it would be you
Standing in the line,
I never thought it would be you
Standing by my side,
But I've never wanted to hurt you
Or girl, see you cry,
I've never wanted for you to be hurt
Until the day I die

I never thought it would be you
Running to my door,
I never even thought in my mind
What you might be there for,
You know I'll love you girl
Forever and evermore
And girl, I'm gonna miss you
When you cast off from my door

Girl, you take my breath away
You mean the whole world to me
And now sitting here by the phone
Waiting for you to call
You know I've known you girl, ever and evermore,
And I'm always gonna miss you when
You cast off from my door

I never thought that we would have
To go our separate ways
I never thought I'd have to deal
With not seeing your face
You know I miss you now more than I've done before
But girl, I'm gonna leave and come running to your door

Girl, you take my breath away,
You mean the world to me
And now that you're gone
The point I struggle to see
You know I've known you girl,
Forever and evermore,

And now I really miss you
Cos you've cast off from my door
I'm always gonna miss you
When you cast off from my door.

Oliver Hudson (13)

Fairytale Song Lyrics

This is no fairy tale with the happily ever after,
This is the one when somebody breaks up.
If it was a fantasy you would cry,
But wipe your eyes, you'll be surprised within the story.
Look at my strength, look at me now,
I used to be somebody who cried out loud,
But I stopped that when I was five.
Now I would love to go back so far because it would be fun,
But now I must go to see what I have done
And make it right to be friends with everyone in this world

Chorus
Everybody in the world will see
That I have changed a lot
And will they do the same?
Come on, come on, you do the same
Come on, come on, you do the same.

This is a fairy tale with the happily ever after
And we will be a little family if we stay the same,
We are sisters and brothers and we have to stick together,
No matter what the consequences are.

We love each other in the same way
So we have to say I love you a lot.

Chorus
Everybody in the world will see
That I have changed a lot
And will they do the same?
Come on, come on, you do the same
Come on, come on, you do the same.

Abigail Monk (9)

27

Reminds Me Of You

When I got that call to say you weren't coming back,
I lost my footing and steered off track.
Nothing feels the same because you're not here,
I feel alone and it's getting worse I fear.
When I call eleven numbers and don't get through,
The voice within, yeah, it reminds me of you.
I push play on my favourite song,
The tune and the lyrics, yeah,
They remind me of you.
I walk down the alleyway and see your ruined car sitting still,
The tears flow through cos it reminds me of you.
I stare at the empty space where you used to lie,
I open the closet filled with the memories,
The ones impossible to buy.
The simple truth I'm scared to admit,
I'm missing a puzzle piece and without it,
Nothing seems to fit.
I don't want to think it's true, you're not really gone,
You're still around the corner,
Cos you promised me you'd always protect me from . . .
The pain that lies inside, the bad times I can't hide,
It's getting difficult to deny,
I promise myself it's all a lie, that you're really gone.
Every day I see your face
And every day I'm missing your embrace,
The memory is disappearing,
But the sound of your name keeps interfering.
But I can't forget you, so I still live this lie,
That you will come back,
Cos you promised you would protect me from,
The pain that lies inside, the bad times I can't hide,
It's getting difficult to deny,
I promise myself it's all a lie, that you're really gone.
I've been trying so hard to wipe my mind,

But what I've realised is, you're one of a kind,
Something special,
Cos although I try to say it isn't true,
Everything I do, reminds me of you.

Kimberley Holdaway (13)

The Marshmallow Song

Chorus
Marshmallow, marshmallows,
Yeh, yeh, yeh, marshmallow,
Marshmallows, yeh, yeh, yeh.

Verse 1
You roast 'em on the fire
You roast 'em on the fire
And then you eat 'em
Then you eat 'em.
You dunk 'em in hot chocolate,
You dunk 'em in hot chocolate
And then you eat 'em,
Then you'll eat 'em.

Verse 2
One marshmallow, two marshmallows,
Three marshmallows, four marshmallows.

Chorus
Marshmallow, marshmallows,
Yeh, yeh, yeh, marshmallow,
Marshmallows, yeh, yeh, yeh.

You roast 'em on the fire
You roast 'em on the fire
And then you eat 'em
Then you eat 'em.
You dunk 'em in hot chocolate,
You dunk 'em in hot chocolate
And then you eat 'em,
Then you'll eat 'em.

Oska Vann (11)

Lies

Being with you was like being in a dream,
a fairytale where you're my knight in shining armour,
you're like a bright star in the sky,
only there was a rush through my body as you gaze into my eyes
When you talk I am hypnotised ...
then I wake up and realise it was all lies
all lies, all lies, all those dirty lies ...
Like magic you changed over night
you used to be so right for me
but you had your chance a ruined it
It's like you're a different person, like you died and went to Hell
or maybe you hit your head and fell
but you've changed in my eyes with all those dirty lies
after that it was like a horror movie
where some innocent person gets hurt
Well guess what, that person was me!
like magic you changed overnight with all those evil dirty lies
and I'm sorry to say that we are through
even though all I wanted was you ...
but all those lies, lies, lies
all those lies, lies, lies
I can see through that mask now
and your true colours are coming through
I am sorry you broke my heart because now you're on your own
we could have been so right together
but obviously it wasn't meant to be
ruined by lies, lies, lies, all those dirty lies, lies, lies
but now I'm the star in the sky
shining brightly through my life
I may not be in a fairytale but I feel like I can fly
because now I'm free to be a star
unlike you, I'm determined to go far
and make something of my life
I won't look back into the past
now I see how it didn't last

time to move on and on forget
all those lies, lies, lies
all those lies, lies, lies.

Rebecca Colwill (14)

Let Go!

I finally believe we were never meant to be,
But you keep having a hold on me,
So we need to let go, let go . . .
I told you I love you and you told me,
But I take it I didn't want you so we need to let go,
But the hold is too strong for me to let go.

But we told each other we'd stay together forever (forever),
So maybe we should save this,
But are you really worth saving and are we really meant to be?
So should we let go, baby should we let go?

We tried to move on, but you couldn't take it anymore
And my heart was torn in two just because of you,
But I take it you love me and I still love you.
So there's no more letting go, cos
I'm not letting go of you now (now).

And now I finally believe we were meant to be,
And there's just a lot of things I would really like to say,
But I guess we'll have to save them for another special day.
We should always be . . .
Together (together) forever (forever).

So there's *no* more fighting and *no* more wars,
No more battling and *no* more hearts torn.
Cos this love is too strong for me to let go, ohhh go,
For me to let go, this love is powerful and rips you into shreds,
But baby there's *no* more fighting, *no* more wars,
No more battling
And baby there's not gonna be a heart torn.
So this letting go is all part of love, please don't let go,
Baby please don't let go.

Lauren Howis (12)

Night Sky

The moon is full
And as blue as a topaz
The sky is black
And as black as can be
Can't you see the stars
Beating through the clouds?

Chorus
This is the night sky
This is the night sky
Beauty like a butterfly
Flying high into the sky
This is the night sky

The sun is down
And it's a starry sky
With the beauty and the darkness
With the darkness in the sky
We will fly high
Into the sky

Chorus
This is the night sky
This is the night sky
Beauty like a butterfly
Flying high into the sky
This is the night sky

The ground is dark
And you can't see the roses
The beauty of the gorgeous rose
Because . . .

Chorus
This is the night sky
This is the night sky
Beauty like a butterfly
Flying high into the sky
This is the night sky.

Elizabeth Raquet (13)

Reality Or What They Didn't Want You To Know

I can't tell you anything, you'll spread it around,
And I can't trust my 'friends', they'll sweep my feet off the ground.
I hide behind laughter, it muffles my fears,
You don't know the real me, never seen my worst fears.

The window to my soul has shattered to pieces,
And you're looking at a face too young for creases, so old.
My soul's so old.
You're looking at a mirror broken so many times,
That the whole damn world has lost all the ties that bind us,
That help to find us . . . oh yeah!

You don't know the feeling and I'm glad for your sake,
How a heart can get hurt and make even you fake.
How a soul can be wrong and ruin your life,
How you can push them all away fearing trouble and strife.

The window to my soul has shattered to pieces,
And you're looking at a face too young for creases, so old.
My soul's so old.
You're looking at a mirror broken so many times,
That the whole damn world has lost all the ties that bind us,
That help to find us . . . oh yeah!

People say I have commitment issues but I say that's untrue,
It's more like I'm people phobic, 'Hey, it's not as if I *couldn't*
like you!'
It's just I'm living in a world that scares me and every day seems
more intense
I'm stuck in an endless fantasy and dreams are clouding my view.

The window to my soul has shattered to pieces,
And you're looking at a face too young for creases, so old.
My soul's so old.
You're looking at a mirror broken so many times,
That the whole damn world has lost all the ties that bind us,
That help to find us . . . oh yeah!

Sophie Hammond (15)

My Perfect Day

When I was little I dreamed of the day,
When a man came along and whisked me away.
I had a great time on my perfect day,
Stood on the beach,
With sand on my feet.

On my perfect day, nothing can go wrong,
On my perfect day,
Wearing my white, frilly dress,
All pretty and pressed on my perfect day.
Looking at my man,
With my ring in his hand,
With the amazing band on my perfect day.
With a grin on his face,
He gives me a wave.

On my perfect day, nothing can go wrong,
On my perfect day,
In his tux,
He gives me those looks
And says he loves me so much on my perfect day.
Puts the ring on my finger,
His love will always linger.

On my perfect day, nothing can go wrong,
On my perfect day,
He looks surprised,
With that look in his eyes,
He says his vows aren't lies,
Bridesmaids at my side,
The sound of the tide.

On my perfect day, nothing can go wrong,
On my perfect day,
That was the wedding,
I will never be dreading,
That I dreamed of when I was little,
It's my perfect day and nothing can go wrong.

Kia Lindley (12)

Best Is Yet To Come

Verse 1
I'm sick of lullabies and deep goodbyes,
Biting from the heart,
Late old nights and stupid fights
Tearing me apart
I can't stay away but you're not the one I want
You keep me here until the day is gone

Chorus
You're just one guy in a list of better
Better yet to come
You're just leaving for the sake of leaving
Scared to be the one
One day I'll turn around and tell you
You're not the one I want

I had stupid dreams from magazines
Screaming to come back
Another girl, another night
Right into the sack
I try to keep you, try to leave you
Today will be the day

Chorus
You're just one guy in a list of better
Better yet to come
You're just leaving for the sake of leaving
Scared to be the one
One day I'll turn around and tell you
You're not the one I want

You see, I tried to help make things right
But I'm not crying
I've already spent too many night
You don't need me
You don't see me
You're just one guy in a list of better
And the best is yet to come.

Aliss Mellar (17)

It's So Sad

V1
I'm looking outta my window
I'm watching the rain fall down
I see your face in front of me
and I feel so, so down

V2
I wonder what you could have been?
a friend a pal or maybe more?
I will never know now will I?
why did you have to go?

Chorus
It's so sad
it's so sad when you lose someone close to you
yeah, it's sad
it's so sad when the feelings are so blue
it's so sad

V3
Ashes to ashes, dust to dust
I hear the priest say
why, oh why did you take that road?
why did it have to end this way?

V4
My friends come and say they're sorry
but they don't really mean it though
I know they never really liked you
but it just goes to show

Chorus
It's so sad
it's so sad when you lose someone close to you
yeah it's sad
it's so sad when the feelings are so blue
it's so sad

wooohh it's soo saaddd.

Rebecca Jayne Roberts (14)

Dreams

A world full of
Imagination and love
Fly over clouds and water
Meet your favourite pop star

Chorus
Cos in your dreams
You can do anything
That you wanna do
Cos in your dreams
You can really live

A universe filled with
Terror and excitement
Swim in hot lava or
Fall in love

Chorus
Cos in your dreams
You can do anything
That you wanna do
Cos in your dreams
You can live

When you dream
Your mind takes over
So keep on dreamin'

Cos in your dreams
You can do anything
That you wanna do
Cos in your dreams
You can live

If you dream on
You'll enjoy it more
Don't stop believin'
Just have fun in
Dreams!

Tayla Gittins (12)

Missing You

I remember that time when I saw your face for the last time,
It was like I never cried so much in my life before,
I know you're watching us.

She had a smile which was so neat,
A voice which was so sweet.
I really miss those times you used to kiss me on my cheek,
I hate it when I hear people say, 'Rest in peace,'
All my heart wants to do is break down and fall to my feet.

Picturing the state of my only mum,
knowing she's lost her older sister
who pushed herself at the age of 51.

Now help me, I've said goodbye
a very special lady
Whose life has just been taken away
And I've grown to realise
appreciate it's your life
that can be taken that day.

You left me with so many messages
scared to hear that you passed
I cried so many tears, so hard it broke my heart!

I've been thinking about all these tragedies
I hope you've been blessing me
but please don't be wasting your time.

Everytime I think away you died,
My chest becomes so tight, I want to break down and cry
Something's really wrong inside ...

Her death, I never thought I'd say goodbye
somebody tell me why
we had to lose you like this?

Her death, I never thought I'd say goodbye
somebody tell me why
we're missing you, we're missing you ...

Gaganpreet Kaur Rura (15)

With You

Verse 1
They keep telling me
To not love in vain
you could feel the pain
And it won't set you free
I could follow their advice
Me and you would never be
Do I do as they say, and be unhappy?

Chorus
But what if they are wrong?
But what if you love me?
This could be the biggest mistake I could make
I just wanna be ... with you
I don't care if it hurts me
I don't care about all the pain
That you may cause me
'cause I just wanna be ... with you

Verse 2
I need to go with my heart
I can't let you go
I just really need to know
That you won't disappear
I can't live with this fear
Maybe I should leave you this now
But I've loved you from the start

Chorus
But what if they're wrong?
But what if you love me?
This could be the biggest mistake I could make
I just wanna be ... with you
I don't care if it hurts me
I don't care about all the pain
That you may cause me
Cause I just wanna be ... with you.

Georgia Perdicou (14)

This Feeling

You have been there, always by my side
When I am so upset, you're the one who keeps me from crying
The tears that fall mean a lot to you
I did not know till I realised that I am in love with you
I couldn't resist it when you weren't there
You're usually far apart but always in my heart
You're the only one who's always making me smile

Chorus
Never knew about this strange feeling
It won't change but it's just that it keeps me
Awake in the night always wondering
About our memories and your smiles, it keeps me thinking
Waiting for your calls and texts like nearly every day and night
It hurts me bad the fact that I can't keep going
It's always keeping me remembering like a little diary
It matters to me when you're not here but there

You're the one always advising and warning me
Already I feel like I've repeated this a million times
My feelings are growing but I'm stuck in the inside
I just never knew it was you this whole time
It's freaking me out though now I can't act or pretend
You're always smiling on, but it keeps this feeling hurrying
If only it just slowed down and just kept me smiling

Chorus
No I never knew
Oh I'm guessing this is it, the truth
It kills me and hurts me bad
But I love the view
Because from where I'm standing, oh I see you
No nothing can stop it, so it's left for us to solve

Chorus

Ooooh – nothing but you and I, can do it.
Well, keep on smiling as this feeling won't be changing.

Shamina Hussain (15)

The Annoying Understood Person!

When I go out the front door of my home
You keep annoying me all of the time . . .
Every time I hide away you seek me from the crowd . . .

Chorus
Because when I see you
I get a shlver down my spine
Because when I hear you
I'm deaf to what you say

When I'm on the beach
You walk beside my right
I make, I make sand sculptures
You trample on them all of the time!

Chorus
Because when I see you
I get a shiver down my spine
Because when I hear you
I'm deaf to what you say

When I'm at the park
I'm on the swing myself!
You sneak up behind me
You push me too high!

Chorus
Because when I see you
I get a shiver down my spine
Because when I hear you
I'm deaf to what you say

When I now see you
I hate you so much
You make such terrible mistakes
You're so scruffy and annoying with every step you take.

Now I understand you with what you do
Now we're a family and our lives are brand new!

Rebecca Kelly (12)

Guilt

A beast in the darkness,
Slashing at my insides,
Red gashes appear,
And all my feeling hide.

I feel it overwhelming me,
I don't know what it is,
As it rattles around inside me,
My head fills with a mist.

It drew a silver, shining blade,
Glittering from tip to hilt,
And as it brought it down on me,
I knew it must be guilt.

I really, really tried,
To recall the things I'd done,
Then finally it hit me,
The race I shouldn't have won.

I knew there must be something,
Something I could do,
I wanted the beast to go away,
I wanted it to shoo.

Then there was a click,
And suddenly I knew,
I knew I had to tell someone,
But who, *who, who*.

Then suddenly I knew,
Who it had to be,
The person who should of won the race,
Harry Hefle-Bee.

As it all gushed out,
And I confessed to all I'd done,
The beast went away,
And I felt like I had won!

Pelham Rhule (11)

Let It Go

Let it go, let it go
We weren't meant for each other
Let it go, let it go
Don't wanna fight again
Let it go
Just let it go

You cheated
You left
You came back
Stop playing games
And

Let it go, let it go
We weren't meant for each other
Let it go, let it go
Don't wanna fight again
Let it go
Just let it go

(Musical break)

When I tell you go
You just stay here
When I call triple 9
You pack up
And
Goooooo

Let it go, let it go
We weren't meant for each other
Let it go, let it go
Don't wanna fight again
Let it go
Just let it go

Oh
Just let it go.

Petros Christoforou (11)

Watch The World Go By

Sometimes life can be
Sometimes life can be tough
Believe me I know
And sometimes people aren't nice at all
But oh, why do I attract that?
When all, all I want to do is sit and watch the world go by

Chorus
Please leave me alone
Just exclude me from it all
I just need some time to think
I'll figure it out
Just gimme some space and time
To watch the world go by
Go by

Verse
I understand that
I understand that things can be tough
Well, don't I know?
But sometimes you just have
Sometimes you just have to; live it out
But why, why do I attract that?
When all, all I want to do is sit and watch the world go by

Chorus
Please leave me alone
Just exclude me from it all
I just need some time to think
I'll figure it out
Just gimme some space and time
To watch the world go by
To watch the world go by
Watch the world go by
Go by
Da, da, da, da, du ...

Harriet Manfield (12)

Last Note

Dance on the dance floor,
Play with sharpened knives,
Before you decipher what is wrong and right,
The terror that lies before you is one you cannot dream,
Dance on the dance floor, until the last note sings.

Will you come with me?
Come on, take my hand, I'll show you everything.

Running around, off our faces, no disgraces (that's right)
No order in our lives, just living our own way.
Follow me if you will, be free, be wild,
Or join the others in the cage, until the last note sings.

When the last note sings,
Dance on the floor,
You cannot dream, the terror that lies before you,
Right and wrong is what you decipher before,
You play with sharpened knives,
And dance on the dance floor.

Will you come with me?
Come on, come on, take my hand,
I'll show you the night and I'll show you the light.

Running around, off our faces, no disgraces (that's right)
No order in our lives, just living our own way.
Follow me if you will, be free, be wild,
Or join the others in the cage, until the last note sings.

When the last note sings,
When the last note sings,
When the last note sings, I'll be waiting.

Running around, off our faces, no disgraces (that's right)
No order in our lives, just living our own way.
Follow me if you will, be free, be wild,
Or join the others in the cage, until the last note sings.

Joe Hollamby (15)

Popularity: A Modest Misnomer

Oh and she said, she said:
'I think I'd prefer life if I could be you,
I think if I could do all the things that you do
I'd hold my head high in my 9 inch shoes.
Then maybe they'd like me too?'

But he said, one day he said:
'We can't all be who we want to be -
I want to go a day without bruising my knees.
But some of us we just live to please,
We're all victims of popularity.'

So sick of doing the things I was told to do,
But then I realised I don't have to . . .

It's my skin, my face, my body, my hair;
The people who matter are the ones who don't care.
They tried to make me look better, ended up feeling worse.
What is popularity but a social curse?

Oh and they said - they said:
'This is going to be how this goes
We know things about you nobody knows'
I hated that they could make me feel so low;
It was then I felt ready to just say, no.

So scared of doing this without you,
But then I realised that I'll pull through.

It's my life, my style, my friends, my clothes,

I really don't care and now everyone knows
That I'm not going to be anything but me now,
So stand back world, it's time you knew how.
It hurts so bad, so bad to walk so tall.
But I'm never, never gonna let them see me fall.
They're never gonna stop and it's gonna get worse -
I'm plagued by idiots in the social curse.

Jordan Preece (15)

Dance Displays!

Walking home from school
Excited for tonight
Shower, dinner and put costumes in the car
On our way, in the car
Feeling pretty nervous
But still trying to act cool.

Walking into the dressing room
Looking for seats
First costume on and make-up done
Saying hi to friends
Practising all my dances
And my heart starting to boom.

People arriving late
Dances being called
I know mine will come along soon
Starting to feel sick
But we're going to be great.

My mum and me watch sister's first dance
She is great
My first dance is called
My friends and I climb the stairs
Feeling even sicker now
But we don't have a second chance.

Just behind the stage
Watching the dance before us finish
Hearing the applause
Curtains shutting, we take our places
Curtains open the music starts
Starting to dance everything is great
The applause tells us we're over
The applause tells us we're over
Walking off the stage, feeling great.

Joanna Ross (13)

47

The Bramall Lane Song

(To the tune of 'Que Sera Sera' by Doris Day)

Saturday has arrived
We're here to keep this game alive
The team will be revealed
When the envelope is unsealed

Chorus
Here we go again
Sat in the pouring rain
Watching our favourite team
We're at Bramall Lane

Cotteril on the wing
Hear the fat men sing
The crowd making up songs
This match seems so long

The referee lost the plot
When Henderson had a shot
Kevin Blackwell shouting
SUFC players mouthing

Chorus
Here we go again
Sat in the pouring rain
Watching our favourite team
We're at Bramall Lane

The usual highs and lows
As the final whistle blows
United win at last
From a left footed blast

As we leave the ground
There are so many fans around
So we've been again
We'll be back to 'The Lane'.

Alfie Sorby (11)

48

Rule The World

You had your fun
You had your chance
Now let us go back
To the time where everybody danced

Let's go to the abandoned park
And sit alone in the tea cups
Under that starry sky
And on a whim we'll decide
That we'll just go rule the world

I once had a dream
That we were dancing on the rings of Saturn
Everyone was watching us
Bowing down at our feet

Let's go to the abandoned park
And sit alone in the tea cups
Under that starry sky
And on a whim we'll decide
That we'll just go rule the world

You were a perverted cat cosplayer
With much on your shoulders
Every night we danced
Under that sky we loved

Let's go to the abandoned park
And sit alone in the tea cups
Under that starry sky
And on a whim we'll decide
That we'll just go rule the world

If I left the dance would you smile?
Or just tell me another lie
We watched the blood boil
Then just walked away.

Lucy Milward (14)

The Demons Feed

Found lost in a lake of fire
I go where only fools fear to tread
You call me only thief and liar
I should have quit while I was ahead
Now you cower from my screams
As I climb higher into the sky
Go destroy your hopes and dreams
Just like me you'll fade and die
My flaws are the only, the only thing left that's pure
You couldn't hate enough to love
So fight the pain that I endure
For now I see you high above

Chorus x 2
As the skies bleed
The demons feed
For Hell is humongous
The Devil's among us
Will we burn if we don't unite?
No we won't cos we will fight

Burn your past and face the truth
Sodomy hides behind the razor blade
You ain't got nothin' so where's your proof?
My eyes bleed black from your disdain
Open your mind, begin to dream
Block the pain with crow-black skies
Watch the Devil and don't blaspheme
Whilst I sit back and scorn your cries
I'll spit you out before I go
For I can control my heat
Then you can rot all alone
Or run away before it's too late

Chorus x 2.

Alex Lacey (16)

An Under-The-Sea Celebration

The sea is crystal clear, a perfect shade of blue,
And the sun's beating down on me and you,
But under the waves on the ocean floor,
There's a whole new world for you to explore,
With colourful corals and golden sand,
Swishing seaweed and a fishy band,
The salmon swing and the jellyfish jive,
And the plaice on the base brings the floor alive!
The carp on the harp and the singing ray,
They're all waiting for you to come and play!

So come join this crustacean concert,
This marine medley,
An underwater wonder, a fish's fantasy!

Look at all the snails that wail, all the little clams that jam,
And the dressed up marlin darlings, with earrings and seashell prams,
Can you hear the eels are squealing?
Watch the lobsters twirl and dance,
Have you seen the minnows' tango?
It can put you in a trance.

So come join this crustacean concert,
This marine medley,
An underwater wonder, a fish's fantasy!

Just look at the starfish salsa, spinning quickly round the floor,
And the lings on strings are catchy,
Their rhythm makes you beg for more!
And the little fish are calling, to us to come dance too,
They've stopped their deep sea celebration,
Just to wait for me and you!

So come join this crustacean concert,
This marine medley,
An underwater wonder, a fish's fantasy!

Liliana Nentcheva (12)

51

My Life!

This is my life, me!
This is who I want to be.

Education bugs me, but education I need.
Goin' out, doin' bad, maybe a laugh,
But another day I've lost,
Losing my dreams.

I gotta little dog,
She's small, too fat.
I've just found out
She's eating me neighbours' scraps.
Some teachers crazy, some I like,
They think I'm dumb,
But my intellect's right.
Then I get in from school,
60 minute make-over,
Oh how I wish that could be true!
But my friend's beside me,
There for good, there for bad.

Education bugs me, but education I need,
Cos the people I look up to
Are the people I want to be.

I wish my family could be back together again,
Don't believe in guns and knives,
They're the things that make the crimes.
I see famous people on the TV and in my mind,
Some of the things I've been through ain't right,
But the rest has been just right.

I know I believe in me,
I know I can get what I want,
I need the right people showing the right way.
One day, I know, one day . . .

Rhys Belcher (12)

The Guy Of Her Dream

I was with my sister one day,
As we walked by
That shop window,
When we saw that guy.

We stopped and stared,
Because we weren't sure
If it was that guy,
My sister adores.

I kept on thinking,
This just can't be,
Where are the paparazzi?
Where could they be?

As he walked
Out of the doors,
I realised it was that guy,
My sister adores.

He looked at her,
She looked at me,
What are the chances,
Of this possibility.

My sister beamed,
This was her dream
To finally greet the guy,
She had longed to see.

She looked at him,
And I could see
That in that second,
There was a spark of chemistry.

They were both so happy,
They were always meant to be.

Emma Leonard (14)

It's The Holiday

The summer holidays are in sight
With just one school week to fight
Whilst temperatures outside are soaring
school doesn't get any more boring!

    Chorus
Oooooooh! Wahoo it's the holiday.
Gonna be great in every way
Wahoo! It's the holiday
everything's gonna be ok!

We hit the road when the holidays start
just wanting to get there is tearing me apart
C'mon c'mon! This isn't fair!
C'mon c'mon! Are we nearly there?

    Chorus

At the beach, not a cloud in the sky
just the fluffy trail of a jet flying by
The sun burning hot on my skin
I'm feeling my suncream wear thin
We play together under the midday sun
The beachball tournament has begun!

    Chorus

We have a beach barbecue after a long, hot day
Hearing the cry of a seagull not far away
The crashing of waves like music to my ears
Washing away all my worries and fears
There's just no need to regret
It's a chance to forgive and forget
cos this time needs no care
and is for everyone to share.

    Chorus.

Laura Knowles (13)

Four Leaf Clover

You were my four-leaf clover
Things were fine till we were over
Now what am I supposed to do?
I'm only lucky when I'm with you

So four-leaf clover, come on over
Come on back, with the luck I lack
Hey, four-leaf clover, come on over
Come on back, with the love I lack

I've never had a lucky charm, no, no, no
Or caught a shooting star fresh from the sky
Nothing ever worked, or seemed to go right
All my dreams just passed me by

Until you came along, yeh, yeh, yeh
You made me feel so free-eee
And I realised what you'd done
You had made me . . . me

So four-leaf clover, come on over
Come on back, with the luck I lack
Hey, four-leaf clover, come on over
Come on back, with the love I lack

I know just what I want
And it's you if you like it or not
Without you I can't go on
You're the reason I stay so strong

So four-leaf clover, come on over
Come on back, with the luck I lack
Hey, four-leaf clover, come on over
Come on back, with the love I lack

So four-leaf clover
Come back over . . . now!

Georgia Hackett (13)

Fishing

Me and my dad went fishing today
And the date was the 5th of May.
Catching lots of fish,
Oh boy, we wish.

Lunchtime came,
We felt hungry the same,
Sitting down to eat our sandwich with Marmite,
And then we got a bite.

We pulled in the rod,
And on the hook was a cod.
This is its make
And now it slithers off into the lake.

The rest of the day was a dull run,
But then there was a ray of sun,
Shining through the grey
And brightening up our day.

Fishing with my dad is great,
He is the one to rate.
My dad has given me lots of tips,
And this has helped me with my blips.

The last fish of the day,
Was a wonderful ray,
Caught on our fishing boat,
Not far from a castle and moat.

Now we have to pack
And put on our macs,
As the rain is on its way,
And I would like to say,

Thank you, Dad, for a wonderful day,
And for being a great mate.

Anna Lawson (13)

Red

Intro
Red is the colour of your lips or the colour of your hair
It's used to warn, it's used to scare
Red is the colour of the rose, the colour of the sun
It's the shade of a war that's just begun

Verse
The tinge upon the horizon
The flame within the fire
I'm told you are the path to Hell
And also the greatest liar
You're laid out as a velvet carpet
Where people walk and pose
I'm torn towards the open door
But then you become the rose

Chorus
Once that colour leaves the rainbow
It spreads itself around so you know
That I'm alive
Shows us what is right or wrong
What's been dangerous all along
That's how I survive

Verse
The healthy look of a baby's face
Or the colour of his hair
Used to warn before danger
Sometimes used to scare
The surface of a rough brick wall
The opening to wound
Shows us you're strong and bold
Proves to us you're doomed.

Chorus.

Ella Heeks (15)

Never Say Goodbye

The first time I saw you there,
I couldn't help but stop and stare,
Now I'm trying to know,
Why you and me we're going slow.

You and me, we're misunderstood,
You seem to think I'm no good,
You don't seem to realise,
That I never want to say goodbye.

Whenever we talk together,
I want the moment to last forever,
When I'm with you I see,
That your heart's reserved for me.

You and me, we're misunderstood,
You seem to think I'm no good,
You don't seem to realise,
That I never want to say goodbye.

Now this is what I just don't get,
We like each other, but you forget,
Will we ever see the day,
When you and me will be okay?

You and me, we're misunderstood,
You seem to think I'm no good,
You don't seem to realise,
That I never want to say goodbye.

I see you looking my way,
We're getting closer day by day.
You and me, we're understood,
Now I realise we're still good.
You finally seem to realise,
That I never want to say goodbye.

Ciara Murphy (14)

Dance So You Can Fall

I've seen the way we live
And I'm thinking we should change
We're all so scared of taking risks
To me it's kind of strange
We always play it safe
Regret what we didn't do
But I'm gonna live my life
And make you live yours too;

You've gotta dance so you can fall
You've gotta sing so you can't talk
Scream and shout for all you're worth
Run and jump till you can't walk

Love until you're broken
All you reckless lovers
Just you keep on loving
We'll live to show the others
Show them how you love
Show them how we dance
Leave no stone unturned
Take every single chance.

You've gotta dance so you can fall
You've gotta sing so you can't talk
Scream and shout for all you're worth
Run and jump till you can't walk

Keep on going round that corner
Just keep on, just keep on going

You've gotta dance, just dance, dance, dance
You've gotta sing, sing all night long
You've gotta shout and laugh out loud
You've gotta run, run all night long.

Landi Wagner (14)

Elope

Verse 1
As I sit down and watch my days
The skies of my life elevates
Up into the sun
The burning flames consume my faith
Try to grab, but shone right in my face
I couldn't save it

Bridge
Sometime the rain of life drowns you immerse
That's that mean I shouldn't try?

Chorus
I built it up
To watch it fall
In the puddle of my fear
I wait and wait
Until the day
I could get the
Courage to away, enthuse my life
Wishing for a ray of hope
But no matter how I try, I have to
Try and elope (3 x)

Verse 2
Through the path of life altercations
Redemption is my salvation
Change is inevitable
The burning picture in glass frame
A glance at the horizon
Is that my fate?

Bridge

Chorus.

Akyaa Boakye-Ansah (16)

This Is Inevitably It

Dewy eyelashes take their final trip past dark, sullen eyes
Streaming hot tears and pouring with tragedy
My heart pounds but my mind wanders . . .
The hypnotic power of such indulgent intoxication and disheartening destruction
To obtain the polished purity of a flawless outcome
Has pulled me into the clasp of its juxtaposed fusion
Suffocating my very being with its refusal to depart.
It seems I am merely leading the life of a manufactured product
Contradicting the fresh, vibrant perspective I have always presented to a culture
So easily misled into an engraved scripture of what has already been done before
Daring not to stray too far from its safety.
However, I am the victim of a robbery whose treasures can never be replaced,
Nor those responsible can be criminalized
And it is this that both inspires and torments me.
As vibrancy rots and reality decays, fantasy flourishes
Peeling back a world in which blunt remarks pierce skin which has not grown so thick
To reveal one in which my naivety is not preyed and gorged upon.
Retreating behind the disguise made for me
My hands tremble as I plead in desperation to remove the disapproval
Defending and denying that I was ever ashamed of who I am.
Can they not understand that bitterness depletes and reaps the world of goodness?
Finding not only solace in my creations
But using them as a tool to relate to those I have always so wished to belong to.
Perhaps protected from fame's concealed complexities
Lulled me into believing a sense of perpetuity had been instilled in my life
But now it seems, this is it, this is inevitably it.

Lucia Curran (16)

Darling

You take my hand I feel OK,
It's dark and cold, but nothing matters either way.
We're walking and talking as my heart beats fast,
We have reached our destination at last.
The train station, the place we go,
a place where only we know.
We sit in the shelter away from the rain,
away from the problems, away from the pain.
Every ten minutes would pass a train,
loud as thunder, clattering of chains.
But still my thoughts are louder,
Still I'm screaming inside,
so still I want to squeeze your hand
and never let this feeling die.
I take in every feature, every detail, every line.
Darling your eyes put the city lights to shame,
you look lovely all the time.
He said, 'Girl, tell me what you're thinking, your eyes,
they look deceiving.'
I said, 'You make me feel like I'm on a ride,
the biggest one of them all,
with no seatbelt, no safety net below me,
incase I drop and fall.
Loads of people are watching,
standing with pride,
I'm even on the telly,
going worldwide.'
He smiled and said, 'I love you too.'
A grand clock stands in front,
strikes a quarter to twelve
but no matter the time, no matter the weather,
there is no limit we've got forever.

Molly McAndrew (15)

Chasing Me

Breathing down my neck again
Break into sweat again
I must confess again
I don't want the stress again
You used to treat me right
Can't stand another night
This game of cat and mouse
Is killing me inside
'Cause you're a stalker
Chasing me
What's it gonna take for you to leave
Me alone?
Go
Get away from me
Get it in your head, my town just ain't
Your home
Last night you followed me
Just like you're taunting me
Everywhere I look I see
You're right behind me
Not like it was before
Can't take it anymore
You used to be my friend
Without a rotten core
'Cause you're a stalker
Chasing me
What's it gonna take
For you to leave me alone?
Go
Get away from me
Get it in your head, this house just ain't
Your home.

Cameron Waghorn (13)

DJ Too Cool For School

Sat here at school looking like a fool,
Yo, yo, I'm too cool for school.
Should have done my homework, wish I had,
No work, yo, yo, I'm too cool for school.
Today it's my birthday,
Feels like my worst day,
Yo, yo, I'm too cool for school.

Here we go again, got a detention,
Never ever had any good mention.
Yo, yo, I'm too cool for school.

Lost my dinner card,
Got done by Mrs Mard,
Yo, yo, I'm too cool for school.

I paid this kid to do my homework,
I was very annoyed,
When I found out he had done no work,
Yo, yo, I'm too cool for school.

Tried out for football,
Said I was too good,
Yo, yo, I'm too cool for school.

Picking me nose,
Biting my toes,
Yo, yo, I'm too cool for school.

Just got an F,
My bird's called Beth,
Yo, yo, I'm too cool for school.

My teacher's shouting,
Because I'm mouthing,
Yo, yo, I'm too cool for school.

George Brooksbank (11)

Loving You Is Hard

I'm still here everyday
Waiting for you to come back
But I'm just so scared
Cos I know it ain't like that

You tell me you love me
Then why the Hell you leave?
I can't live without your love
It's making my heart bleed

I thought you cared for me
I thought you was gonna
Always be there for me

You're the only person
I wish I could forget about
Cos I know it's over without a doubt

One min I hate you
The next I still love you
I don't know what to do
You broke my heart in two

I don't understand
Why you changed your mind so suddenly
Was it me or was it you?
Cos I don't have a clue

I love you and I'm waiting
For you to come back
But I don't think it's
Gonna end up like that

You're the only person
I wish I could forget about
Cos I know it's over without a doubt.

Siân Llewellyn (14)

If Only

If only
You could see all you meant to me
Some people aren't meant to be
But baby, that's not you and me.

You had my heart
But all you did was break it in half
Now we're not even friends
Will we ever speak again?

And it's colder now than ever
There's just some storms I cannot weather
I need you there by my side
Telling me everything's alright.

If only we could be together
Meant to be forever and ever
We could make it OK
It was never meant to be this way.

If only, oh
If only
If only

Now the clouds have gone away
I can see clearly again
But baby it's just not the same
I need to see you again

I'm sorry
For everything I didn't see
It's impossible to forget
Always live with this regret

If only, if only, oh, oh
If only, if only, if only, if only . . .

Judith Allen (13)

Come Back To Me

Verse
Oh, yeah,
Every day I try to play another game,
But I just can't take it,
Try to find another guy, oh
Why can I not shake it?
My heart is broken into two
Oh, I just can't get over you
I don't know why,
You're just that perfect guy (hold)
Yeah.

Chorus
Oh, come back to me,
I know that we should be
Oh baby, come back (hold),
When we first met, I knew
We had some connection,
I need protection,
So come back (hold)
To me. Oh (x2)

Verse
You're always on my mind,
You give me signs that you're the one,
I knew we had something,
Now you left me with nothing.
Ohh! My heart is broken
Into two. I don't know what do
Do (hold). Yeah.

Chorus x 2 (second time rap).

End - please come back to me.

Bethany Lloyd (14)

School Time Rap

Clip, clap, ping, ping,
School bell *ring, ring.*
Clip, clap, ping, ping,
Time for my thing.

I'm walking out of school,
Everything's cool,
I'm with my mates,
They're so great!

Clip, clap, ping, ping,
School bell *ring, ring.*
Clip, clap, ping, ping,
Time for my thing.

Down the stairway,
Mr Day,
House meeting, so boring,
My head's leaning, nearly snoring!

Clip, clap, ping, ping,
School bell *ring, ring.*
Clip, clap, ping, ping,
Time for my thing.

Clock's ticking, so am I,
Looking out the window, at the sky,
School work's boring! Why, oh why?

Clip, clap, ping, ping,
School bell *ring, ring.*
Clip, clap, ping, ping,
Time for my thing.
Clip, clap, ping, ping,
Clip, clap, ping, ping!

Carly Booth (11)

Leave Me Alone

Verse 1
Every day
I try to open my heart
To somebody else
But it doesn't work
So I need you to leave me alone
Please . . .
(Hum, hum, hum x 2)

Chorus
So I'm saying to you
Leave me alone
I can't stand you near
So get away from here
The flowers are faded now
So just leave me alone

Verse 2
I've tried to tell you this before
But you didn't seem to get it
So I've written this song just for you
And I hope you'll understand now
So I need you to leave me alone
Please . . .
(Hum, hum, hum x 2)

Chorus
So I'm saying to you
Leave me alone
I can't stand you near
So get away from here
The flowers are faded now
So just leave me alone.

Rebecca Portas (11)

I'm Sweet But I'm Sour

I'm sweet but I'm sour,
Can't make myself better,
Don't care if you hate it,
I'll be like this forever,
I'm sure I can do this,
So I will just be me,
That's all I'm gonna do,
It's what I want to be!

I'm sweet but I'm sour,
You should know that now,
I've always been like this,
It's like I don't know how,
To break up my sourness,
To balance my sweetness,
I can't because that's how I am!

I'm sweet but I'm sour,
That's why I play the game,
Don't know what to do,
To get back into fame,
Trying to be normal,
As it's how I will be,
I know what to do,
Just you wait and see!

I'm sweet but I'm sour,
You should know that now,
I've always been like this,
It's like I don't know how,
To break up my sourness,
To balance my sweetness,
I can't because that's how I am!

Ellen Roberts (12)

My Mum's Sad At Me

My mum's sad at me
I didn't wanna do homework tonight
I've gotta go out and play
She's so angry with me
Why doesn't Mum see?
I don't like her angry
But I need to go out
And play football with my mates
Then stay up till ten!

My mum's sad at me
We've been shouting for the last hour
It got very loud
I really, really hate arguing with her
Why is it this way?
Why does she always say
That all the things I play
Are a waste of time?
I should be working hard
Not out with my mates.

My mum's sad at me
We argue every night
We nearly got it sorted
She argued with what I said
I knew it was tense
I thought I could just go out
Now when I try to talk
She says I'm a waste of space
She says I'll lose my place
Now she says I'm grounded

My mum's sad at me!

Joe Cannings (11)

Sucker For Love

I guess I was stupid, I guess I was dumb
But now I know you're not the one
I don't understand why you broke my heart
All I know is that I'm torn apart
My girls told me, 'Don't, he's not right'
Man, I should have listened because I'm crying all night
I really did love him and I still do
I don't care if that makes me a fool
I was gonna make you my baby, more than a friend
Why did you say this had to end?

Well, I must be a sucker for love
Someone help me, I've had enough
I keep crying like it's my daily routine
And I hate to think that you used me
Well, I must be a sucker for love

Why do the ones I love always leave?
Is it because you think I'm a tease?
If you do, I'll change for you
Just tell me, will you think it through?
I keep thinking about when we kissed
Please don't tell me this is it
I never really cry over a boy
But I cried over you and I'm not a toy
I do have feelings
But it's your face I can't stop seeing.

Well, I must be a sucker for love
Someone help me, I've had enough
I keep crying like it's my daily routine
And I hate to think that you used me
Well, I must be a sucker for love

Merces Teixeira (13)

The World

Butterflies flying in their own little way
Gracefully fluttering about
From a small little caterpillar
To a pretty little butterfly

The world is such a wonderful place to be
The world is such a beautiful place to see
You can't find anywhere better
Than the world
The world

Blue sky's silent breeze
The sun glimmering in the sky
Children running in the park
Flowers and trees gently waving
The smell of smoking barbecues wafting about
It makes everyone crazy

The world is such a wonderful place to be
The world is such a beautiful place to see
You can't find anywhere better
Than the world
The world

Dolphins twirling around in the sea
Fishes swimming around peacefully
Waves calmly hitting against the rocks
The sun beams down and seagulls fly

The world is such a wonderful place to be
The world is such a beautiful place to see
You can't find anywhere better
Than the world
The world.

Jessica Garfield (10)

Love Isn't All It Seems

Nerves and the butterflies,
And everything is going fine,
First time, to fall in love,
So sure that he's good enough.

Tears and the smiles,
Emotions are all running wild,
The hurt and the pain,
When the feelings don't stay the same.

Chorus
And we fall,
Way too fast,
Sometimes the
Love don't last,
So much faith,
So much belief,
Sometimes we are deceived,
Love isn't all it seems.

Glances and hidden stares,
Pretending that you don't care,
Sleepless nights and trying to find,
The strength just to be alright.

The hoping and the healing,
And then it's light that you're seeing,
First time, second time,
And then the pain is suddenly fine.

Love isn't always,
The same as our dreams,
Because love isn't always,
All that it seems.

Mehvish Rehman (14)

What Did You Get?

I'm just a kid
Sat here at school
Really, really bored
Leaning on my stool

Listening to my teacher
Rabbiting on and on
Why am I here?
It's just at home I wanna be

What did you get?
Maths - I got a D
What did you get?
Science - I got a C
What did you get?
Spanish - I don't really wanna say

Oh ooh
I only wanna be at home
Then my teacher says it's up to me
I'm really confused

Who am I?
What can I be?
I just wanna speak out loud
Just to be free

What did you get?
History - I got an E
What did you get?
Music - I got an F
What did you get?
English - I don't wanna say
What did you get?

Megan Godbehere (12)

Separated

I've never felt so alone,
Separated by faces I've never known,
Wishing I was there with you,
But I'm all alone.

Drowning in my tears,
Consumed by all my fears,
Alone in this world without you,
Don't think I can go on like this.

Time ticks by,
Every minute goes so slow,
When I'm with you time seems to fly,
But now I'm all alone.
People used to tell me,
This is the real world kid,
So you should get used to it.
I never listened till now,
And now I know it's true.

Drowning in my tears,
Consumed by all my fears,
Alone in this world without you,
Don't think I can go on like this.

Drowning in my tears,
Consumed by all my fears,
Alone in this world without you,
Don't think I can go on like this.

But I'm all alone now,
I'm without you somehow,
I'm all alone now,
I'll have to get by (whispered) somehow.

Cariad Morgan (16)

Swept Away

Verse 1:   I'm feeling my way through the dark
With no purpose and no aim
Shapes blur in front of my eyes
What is it I'm searching for?
Would I even recognise?

Pre-chorus: The pages keep turning
I'm going too fast
Dragged under by the current
And I'm swept away by life

Chorus: How can I search if there's nothing to find?
How could I lose if there's nothing to win?
How will I think if I've lost my mind?
Lost in memories
Living in strife
Is it not time I moved on?
Or I'll be swept away by life

Verse 2:   Heads of strangers turn around
Just to see what they missed out
Oh, but it's far too late
Can you pray if you've lost your faith?
What do you believe?
Chorus

Bridge: The current's getting stronger
Somehow the weak survive
Have you been deluded?
Oh, how can you be sure?
When nowhere is home for you anymore
Chorus
Swept away
Swept away
By life.

Alice Watts (15)

Let Go!

My freedom, my choice
My personality, my voice
You suck it out of me, all right out of me
You suck it out of me, all right out of me
Into the fiery pits of Hell
That awful and wretched smell
You suck it out of me, all right out of me
You suck it out of me, all right out of me
I have no choice anymore
You've all got to go (oh no! (Add evil laugh))
Get away from me
Get out of my face
I need my space
Just go away
There's only one way!
I'm running away from you, running away from you
Moving away from you, far from you
Hope you don't find me
And never come near me
It's me and him
Not me and you anymore, (anymore (echo))
I'm going away because
You suck it all out of me, all right out of me
You suck it all out of me, all right out of me
I have no choice, you got to go
It's either you or me
Or me or you
There will be only one survivor. Me! Because I'm the fighter
You suck it all out of me, all right out of me
You got to go
The end!

Mandeep Bal (16)

Too Late

Left on the streets to die
Locked up inside their murdered minds
Oh how I despair, cos we don't even care
Don't be a second too late
Who knows how long we've got to live?
With all the killing and fighting
We are losing sight of who we are.
So don't be a second too late
Who knows how long we've got to give?
With all the traffic and lighting
We are losing sight of who we are.
So when I tell you what a state this planet's in
Do you ever stop to think it could be over in a blink?
So don't throw your life away
Do something good today.
Don't be a second too late
The killing and fighting must stop here
Don't leave people to die
We're all the same inside
Who knows how long we've got to live?
Prevent starvation
It could be over in a blink
Whoa yeah
Don't be a second too late
Who knows how long we've got to live?
With all the killing and fighting
We're losing sight of who we are
So don't be a second too late.
Who knows how long we've got to give?
With all the traffic and lighting
We're losing sight of who we are.

Rhian Pearce (12)

Fifteen Minutes Of Fame

Gazing back at her forlorn reflection,
Analysing the dark circles etched along her papery complexion,
A woman of delusion is presented
Dilapidated and tormented
Face for fame decayed,
Within the notorious and star-studded place
Jealous tipped tongue of envy they display
Each living within her magical reality
Her life a prosthetic place of superficiality
Privileges of privacy prevented
Paparazzi hunting the tormented
Nosey journalists linger and dance
The brutality of their entangled lies enhanced,
Keep her afraid and helplessly paralysed
Against the enduring scrutiny
Of the public's enquiring eyes
Her trembling fingers graze her once magnificent features
The ones which catapulted her to fame and diamond encrusted dentures
As the callous claws of narcissism
Leave fingerprints of criticism
Imprinted along the contours of Miss Self-conscious
His eyes displaying a look of indulgence
Rhythmic cackles penetrate the ears of the weak,
His laughs reverberate and creak,
Fame, a thwarted place
A vicious and undignified chase,
Toward the ultimate podium of superstardom
Average Joe's yearning for their limited recognition
Their thirst for the ridiculous, becoming an obsession
Disregarding the concealed squalor and fifteen minute infamy,
Swallowed up in a world of temptation and instability.

Jacqueline Duven (18)

I'm Sorry

I'm sorry for all the wrong I've done,
Sorry to lose the songs we've sung,
If I'd known that it would do you harm,
I swear I'd never have done it at all.
The times we shared, are now all gone
Things we said, all forgotten
I sit here by your hospital bed
And I watch you slip away
Away over the hills
Back where we used to play
In the sun, every day
Who knew we'd end up this way
I've always loved you,
Don't ever forget that!
It's who I am . . .
You're a part of me,
You always will be, you're my right half.
I needed someone to steady me, it was you
When you had a rough time, I tried to do what I could
It's not easy, try to be happy, do it for me,
I hate seein' you with your face drawn and gaunt
I think of that cancer, eatin' away at your heart
And I'm . . .
I'm sorry for all the wrong I've done
Sorry to lose the songs we've sung
You're my candle in the dark
I'm just the body, but you're the heart . . .
I'm sorry for all the wrong I've done
Didn't mean to cause you harm
Don't want you to leave me
But you have to go on . . .

Attiyyah Omerjee (16)

Apathy Is Fear

The thud of the clock
Matches the beating of my heart
The wind in the trees
Matches a strum on my guitar

If time speeds up, my thoughts slow down
Head full of air, I nearly drown

The sound of my beating heart
Drowns out the screams
They're dying outside, but I can't part
With the shadows of my dreams

The steps on the pavement
Remind me of marching to a beat
The blurred lights we pass
Remind me of fire in the streets

Volume goes up, the screaming stops
The heat is on, the temperature drops

The sound of my beating heart
Drowns out the screams
They're dying outside, but I can't part
With the shadows of my dreams

Save me, save me, save me from myself
Turn the focus onto someone else
Look at the new idol in HD
I can ignore the problem that is me

The sound of my beating heart
Can't drown out the screams
Dying inside, I should part
With the shadow that is me.

Theres Lessing (15)

Destiny

Verse 1
I miss you every moment of the day you ain't here
With you by my side I had nothing to fear
You meant everything to me, so why'd you have to go?
Now that you left me, I'm feeling pretty low
So tell me what's the issue
You know that I miss you
I would never try to diss you
Only try to kiss you
You know that I love you
No one is above you
You're beautiful like a dove too
And I can't get enough of you

Chorus
Because I know we are meant to be
You're the only one for me
Baby now can't you see
You and me are destiny, destiny, destiny
You and me are destiny

Verse 2
I don't blame you for giving up hope
Without you by my side I don't think I could cope
I can't live without you
I love everything about you
From your hair to your legs and your height that is 5'2"
You are clever, you are gorgeous
When I see you, you are flawless
Without you I am coreless
Together we are lawless
Now it's time for the chorus.

Louie Bloom (13)

Walk Away

I can see right through your act,
Don't pretend you don't know,
That you've struck my heart,
I'll try to ignore the impact, but
The more and more I try,
The harder it is not to cry.

I won't let the flames burn my heart,
Never again will you tear me apart,
Though my heart's been cracked in two,
I know I'll be fine without you.
Just walk away, and don't turn back,
Before everything fades to black.

Didn't know you'd become the enemy,
Feels like your surrounding me,
Didn't want to have to put up a fight,
But it seems like I just might
Have to tear you apart,
So you can see,
Exactly what you did to me.

I won't let the flames burn my heart,
Never again will you tear me apart,
Though my heart's been cracked in two,
I know I'll be fine without you.
Just walk away, and don't turn back,
Before everything fades to black.

I'm just gonna walk away ...
Tomorrow's another day so
Even if we have to fight,
I think it's gonna be alright ...

Katy Shortt (13)

Wait

It's 3am, I'm yet to sleep,
I'm starting to think I'm in too deep,
Tonight's the third night I'll see tick through
I'm too busy losing sleep over you
Is my timing off, did I miss my chance?
The song is over before I asked you to dance.

Step on stage, you were born to play this part,
I'll be the cliché, you'll be the boy who breaks my heart,
The script is saying - the next line is goodbye,
But I'll take the leap and improvise.
I know I should move on, I know I should forget,
But I'm not willing to give up on you just yet.
I'd wait forever, and then I'd wait for you.

I scan the crowd, but now you're gone,
These blank faces just remind me you're the one,
I've fallen for you, I must confess,
I don't know how I got into this mess,
I couldn't call my own bluff,
When I said I'd never fall in love.

Step on stage, you were born to play this part,
I'll be the cliché, you'll be the boy who breaks my heart,
The script is saying - the next line is goodbye,
But I'll take the leap and improvise.
I know I should move on, I know I should forget,
But I'm not willing to give up on you just yet,
I'd wait forever, and then I'd wait for you.

I'd wait forever,
And then for you,
Forever, I'd wait for you.

Victoria Green (16)

My Broken Heart

Remember the first time you looked at me
I knew you were the one.
After all these years, I'm so alone.
My heart no longer wants to beat,
Look what you've done to me
Why have you left me in so many pieces?

I still think of you
Come back to me and
Help mend my broken heart

I can feel you there, standing alone
You feel the same, hurt and pain
I wanna be with you, don't you see
Come back to me and
Help mend this heart you once broke

This heart is yours, it longs for you, it cries for you
So come back and
Mend my broken heart

I lay awake, all alone
I hear all these whispers telling me to let go
It's not that easy
I've been holding onto this pain too long
I don't want to let go
Nor do I want to be alone

You were my brightest light but
You've become my darkest fear
So, come back and
Mend this heart you once broke

My broken heart . . .

Riya Chauhan (18)

My Buddies

They always stand beside me,
Forever and to the end.
They help me through the good and bad,
My wonderful, amazing friends.

Becky, she is so funny,
Even when it's not meant to be.
She's been my mate since we were three,
We're chained together and have no key.

Rhianna, wow! What a friend!
She listens to what you've got to say.
She gives advice on how to solve problems,
She's there for me, every day.

Holly, she never stops smiling,
She's always on the go.
So petite, but such a big heart,
She's a lovely person to know.

Georgia, so well behaved,
She does great in class.
She spends a lot of time abroad,
The lucky, lucky lass!

Emily, our little 'hardnut'!
The tomboy of our clan.
Girls beat boys at football?
Our Emily can!

We are all different shapes and sizes,
And have different interests for a start!
We are brought together, through friendship
And will never be apart.

Bethany Woodcock (12)

Will It Change?

The world is full of corrupt elections
Vengeful leaders attempt to seek perfection
In this cold world where young troops are falling
Life has gone gory like one of the Devil's drawings

The world has changed into a living nightmare
Where people are suffocating looking for air
The government sending youths to fight
Knowing well they won't come back to see the light

Why are there world wars, are they to settle peace?
Peace is non-existent if the firing don't cease
They choose not to listen they got an itchy trigger finger
Once they let go the smell of dead bodies will linger

Many people are out there grieving and dying
They're looking to the government but they're not supplying
The government use their power beyond its limitation
They don't use that power to feed an African nation

People are out there, get killed for no reason
Question God in some countries, you'll get burned for treason
President Mugabe slaughtering millions of lives
But he don't think about young children of wives.

Young kids live in denial, feel safe carrying knives
They're just scared to face themselves, they're feeling demise
The world carries so many hidden truths and lies
To find them all, we have to open our minds

Why do people turn a blind eye to world?
It makes my brain think, question and unfurl
Salvaging through my mind and I'm trying to find
The answer for life, but I think I'm going blind.

Jay Patel (15)

88

This Place

I know this place,
I've been here before,
You used to love me so much,
But not anymore.

This place reminds me,
Of what we used to be,
Just us, in our own little world,
Forever, you and me.

But now you've gone,
You've run away to the other side,
I can't face it any more,
All there is to do is hide.

All my memories,
Have come flooding back,
I have to leave this place,
My world is turning black.

As much as I try,
I cannot hide,
From the past that haunts me,
I still feel it inside.

If only it were as easy,
As black and white,
Would we still remember,
Would we still fight?

Remember us, together,
Remember you and me,
Forever, forever,
Forever, you and me.

Molly Williams (12)

Seasons

The winter flower awakens,
Moving through the ground,
Ready to slowly burst out,
Spring has begun,
Its petals start to seek out the sun,
The roots start to become more secure,
Would this preparing spring ever end?

It spreads its petals as far as it can reach,
Enjoying the beautiful sunshine,
Summer had begun,
Bees are buzzing around,
Ready to feed on its yellow pollen,
Its leaves are greener than ever,
Would this glorious summer end?

Slowly this plant starts to die,
Getting smaller and smaller,
Autumn has begun,
Only a little flower is left, trying to fight for its life,
Eventually all the petals will fall in the harsh wind,
The flower knows it's time to go underground,
Would this crisp autumn ever end?

Still the plant is trying to survive,
It sinks back into the ground,
Where it is cosy and warm,
Winter has begun,
The bulb curls up,
Drifting to sleep,
Ready for the spring,
Hoping this freezing winter would end.

Poppy Wynn (11)

Airhead

Another fashion magazine,
Another anorexic teen,
Skipping her lunch and makin' herself vomit,
Her parents think she's being bullied, but the truth is far from it.

She wants to be a supermodel, just like Kate Moss,
Sitting in class putting on her make-up thinking she can just doss,
I've seen a million and one of these kind of girls,
More interested in straightening their hair and getting rid of their curls.
That girl thinks she's got to be something clone-like,
Her and her friends just sit there laughing at the class dyke,
Another fashion magazine,
Another anorexic teen,
Skipping her lunch and makin' herself vomit,
Her parents think she's being bullied, but the truth is far from it.

When she was younger they told her she could go far,
That she was one of the brightest, could be a superstar,
Now every day she drinks and she'll smoke,
Wasting away her life, but it won't matter,
As long as she isn't the centre of the joke,
Plastered in blusher and foundation,
Is this what really comes of the girls of our nation?
Another fashion magazine,
Another anorexic teen,
Skipping her lunch and makin' herself vomit,
Her parents think she's being bullied, but the truth is far from it.

Another fashion magazine,
Another anorexic teen,
Skipping her lunch and makin' herself vomit,
Her parents think she's being bullied, but the truth is far from it.

Chloe Arnold (14)

Cold

I'm cold.
My heart used to be so warm.
Such a long time ago
When there was something like me and you.

I'm gone. Far apart,
We're alone and forgotten.
The light has gone, darkness rules,
There's only a gaping hole
Where you once were.
In my heart there's a space
Where you used to be,
Now I wonder and I pray,
Do you still remember me?

We made that promise oh, so long ago
That we'd be together
Against the world,
For always and forever,
Now I'm cold.

Now without you
I have nothing to hold onto,
There's no one there to hold me when I cry,
There's no one there to help me fly,
I'm cold.
I'm alone and forgotten,
Holding tight,
To a hope so bright,
That my winter will end,
With the return of a friend
And I won't be so cold.

Charlotte Buchan (15)

Baby Baby

You gave me a feeling like no other
you gave me a look oh, just another
you gave me a smile and turned around
and there you were standing in the crowd and said,

'Baby, baby you're the one
baby, baby oh, I'm going so numb
baby, baby can I have a chance?
baby, baby may I have this dance?'

You looked at me and I tingled inside
I knew something was gonna happen tonight
it may be just a silly fling
but I hope you really sing,

'Baby, baby dance with me tonight
baby, baby this feeling's so right
baby, baby will you give me a twirl?
baby, baby will you be my girl?'

Tonight is coming to its end
It's to decide if we're more than just friends
I really think I like you a lot
so can we give it a shot?
and I said,

'Baby, baby yes you're the one
baby, baby oh, you're making me numb
baby, baby you took your chance and
baby, baby you can
have this dance
baby, baby you're liking my whirl
baby, baby now I will be your girl!'

Molly Banyard & Lauren Marley (13)

Wings

Chorus
Give me wings so I can fly, fly, fly away
away from the violence away from the pain
to a place that I'm loved with the ones that I love
please give me my wings and let me fly

Verse1
I come home from school round about four
all I hear is shouting and screaming
my daddy's yellin' my momma's cryin'
another big fight 'bout another small thing
so I dump my stuff, change my clothes and go
gotta get outta here, get away from this place

Chorus

Verse2
My escape it don't last that long
gotta go home and face the music
I walk in the door and wham goes his fist
he hits my face throws me against the wall
I run upstairs and look in the mirror
gotta find a better way to escape this place

Chorus

Verse3
I've found my escape but I'm scared
to take my life is the only way
then I'll have my wings to make me fly high
he won't hurt me no more, I'll be gone forever
no one will miss me because no one cares
I'll close my eyes forever tonight, I'll be happy this way.

Rebecca Morris (14)

We Don't Say Hello (Anymore)

In the rush of lonely people,
Wishing to say hello,
Walking through lonely streets,
With nothing much to do.

They long to spare a hug or two,
But simply pass on by,
Cos they wouldn't know what to say,
Their excuse is there's no time.

I used to know my best friend,
But she's passed on by,
Another face in the sea of names,
Because she doesn't have the time.

Well, maybe in the land of go,
You might not know my name,
But I'm sure if you just stopped still,
You'd be the one to blame.

I used to know my best friend,
But she's passed on by,
Another face in the sea of names,
Because she doesn't have the time.

You used to know your best friend,
Who was always you,
You wake up in the morning
And say hello ego.
If self-centred wasn't so harsh,
I'd use it to describe (you),
Cos I used to know my best friend
And believe me, it ain't you.

Evie Charlesworth (16)

Doubt

The doubt of a mind
The search for perfection
Beyond the mirror's reflection
Which path to choose
Hurt those who love you
Or love those who hurt you
A questioning ... endless and listless
Circling round and round
The turn into the unknown
Lost in the wilderness
A lonely road ahead
A cloud looming over the bed
The shrug and forlorn frown
The silent silence
Echoes around a room
Like a floating feather
Time slowly deceasing as it settles to the floor
The uncertainty of an atom
Or even a molecule
Emotions maybe
Straining at the strings of the heart
Maybe to doubt hides the person within
A shelter for the homeless soul
Or even an escape from the real world
To be driven away
But as the sand timer
Bears the last grain of pale yellow sand
The escape distorted from
The never ending shadow of
Doubt.

Emily Cox (18)

Mad Public Transport

I'm a survivor
So give me a fiver
Get on a bus and shoot the bus driver
I thought it was funny
I took all his money
The next day I got in a taxi
I left so soon cos the driver was nasty
So I went to the bus station
I saw the bus that runs the whole nation
They ran - they didn't want to get shot
But the driver was so flamin' hot
I drove down to the chippy that was nice
I found a limo reserved for Katie Price
So I went down to the ferry
They wouldn't let me on it - it was reserved for Katie Perry
So then I went to catch a train
But I thought it would be quicker to go by plane
It's funny how I landed in Spain
It would have been better to travel by train
So I went down to the southside sea
But all the bus drivers tried to shoot me
I tried to travel by car
But after an hour I hadn't gone far
So then I travelled by a black cab
It was boring but I thought it would be fab
So I entered an amazing tour bus
But all the famous people tried to kick a fuss
They threw me off the top deck and I thought I broke my neck
A man said, 'Hop in, come for a roam'
I went round the corner and ended up home.

Chris Wilson (13)

Soaring Rapture

As if propelled by wind, triggered by such unearthly concepts
Rising and falling with gusts and breaks
Then almost falling, but merely pausing
The wings of this butterfly flutter with urgency
Such a natural being, yet unearthly power controls
With the silence of a burning flame, flickering
Almost extinguished but again lit
Fuelled by the oil of love and anger
A rainbow of colours when illuminated
A slick darkness when in shadow
Each beat fuelled by love and hate
One cannot know one without the other, cannot be
What is blind hate without all consuming love
Flickering, fluttering back and forth
Moving to the repetitive yet vital tune of a throbbing heart
Full of life yet also the key to survival
An invisible mechanism, each part working in unison
Controlling the seemingly constant elevation
Such inconceivable power, drawing one wing to the other
Each face a mirror of the other, each face working off the other
This fragile paper cut-out, so violently alive
Soaring through the clear spring air
Forging on through harsh autumn winds
No heavy drops falling from above can crush it
No water can extinguish the flame
Propelling forward through the velvety darkness of the future
So alluring yet truly frightening
Propelling forwards forever to find its way
The essence of the gentle and invisible
The powerful desire to survive and conquer all.

Emma Mann (19)

I Miss You Baby, I Miss You Maybe

I'm gonna break the silence
And tell you that I miss you
And all the times that we laughed until 2am
About nothing that anyone would understand but us
And I remember what it feels like
To be the only one you want to be with
And the one you only ever wanted to be with
But what do we have to show
For everything we did together
And the times we spent together?
I miss you, baby
I miss you, maybe
The message in a bottle
Telling you that I love you
But do you feel that way too
Or do you just want to give up on us?
Do you think it's too late
Are we just fighting in a losing battle
Or do we have a hope of winning?
But what do we have to show
For everything we did together
And the times we spent together
I miss you baby
I miss you maybe
Do you ever think about how I am
And ever want to pick up the phone to say
I miss you baby
I miss you maybe
Yeah, I miss you baby
I miss you baby?

Michaela Mullett (14)

I've Got No Luck!

I'm sitting in class
Doing my maths
The teacher yells
Miss Wells
1, 2, 3
I've got no luck
4, 5, 6
Your shirt's untucked
Why, why do I have to work?
She says it gives me a perk
1, 2, 3
I've got no luck
4, 5, 6
Your shirt's untucked
Walking home full of glee
I say so long teachee
Miss Wells' detention!
I won't get a special mention
1, 2, 3
I've got no luck
4, 5, 6
Your shirt's untucked
Sitting in my seat
Having a bite to eat
Miss Wells, 'What are you eating?'
'Nothing Miss, just sleeping.'
1, 2, 3
I've got no luck
4, 5, 6
Your shirt's untucked.

Abbie Mitchell (11)

The Road To Heartbreak

I'm not the girl who got her heart broken
That's what I tell myself inside my head
I wish we could rewind we should have spoken
So many words that night were left unsaid
They say love's a game but it's never fair
Play by the rules but get nowhere
Hoped we would have bypassed that part
And been as good as we were at the start
My mind's confused, heart torn in two
Can't eat or sleep this is untrue
I'm strugglin', too weak to win
This got too deep, something we couldn't keep
Why couldn't I see
That this love was going to kill me?
'Cause when we drifted apart
The magic died along with my heart
Now I just feel this vast pain
Tears I cry lost out in the rain
All that's left is a memory
Of how perfect we used to be
Why . . .
Why did our relationship get out of hand?
The fighting and the rumours were not what I'd planned
I'll try to live life without you
But if I fall what will I do?
My heart can't take this
I've got to let go
This is the final show
I guess this is goodbye
Feels like I'm gonna die.

Whitney Donaldson (14)

The Elements Of You

You crashed like a hurricane through my doors
Smashed my sparkling eyes to diamond shards
Ripped my foundations clean to the floor
Yet, when the wind died; I came crawling for more.
You threw me more chances than a loaded die
but offered more raises than I could give
meddled the cards and hid the jacks
But you know your deft hands are my secret stack.
You offered more fire than a burning gun
Passion exploding through shadowy dreams.
Breaking my heartbeat with the whip of a bullet
I'm entranced, locked at the end of the mullet.
You gave me the spark to light up my eyes
But threw in the gasoline to drench them first.
Igniting my dusty, cracked porcelain ideals,
of a smoking black heart with a kiss for a seal.
You cracked open a star and fed me the dust
molten gold moments rushing into my veins
Sparkling, crystallising, burning my thoughts
Just when I thought I couldn't burn anymore.
You stole my thunder with your bare hands
Lighting the dawn for a pretty young thing
A romantic understudy to fill in my story
Of a lovelorn girl with lightning bolt fury
You tore my sky free from its silvery seam
Letting my gravity merge with the heavens
Footloose and lone, a rest on a star
I watch the clouds burn; we've lost where we are.
So I held your smile at ransom and hung it on my lips
Praying for the courage to abandon this sinking ship.

Jenny-Rose Kendrick (17)

The Truth Only He See's

He is looking out to space, but I can see through his glare
It's not intentional, only a subconscious mistake
You can see it in his eyes right there
His interests revolve around the same thing
You wealthy people might not understand it
That something so small holds his attention but
It holds uncertainty and his mind seems square
Absolutely nothing familiar about it
When she comes around, the world is one big sound
You see, she's nothing special but
You can't see what he can see
And I know it may seem odd, but
Nothing makes sense in this racket
You say, 'God save the Queen' and he thinks *God save her*
He says, 'She's completely faultless', misleading but forgivable
Unhidden secrets that she can't show
Her only vice is her own shadow
When she comes around, the world is one big sound
You see, she's nothing special, but
He can't see what we see
And I know, it may seem odd, but
He can't see her shadow in the dark
Yeah in the dark
When all his thoughts form into one
Can't read her face, next thing she's gone
She's the missing piece to his torn up puzzle
But one that can't be found
And I know, it may seem odd, you see
She's nothing special, but
We can't see what he can see.

Bethany Charlton (14)

103

The Game Of Life

Life is like a game, it can be easily won
But once you start the game you have to play till it's done
You can be serious or just play for fun
Either way you have to play just like everyone
Life can be won by achieving success
Some people don't settle for anything less
All you have to do is just try your best
Or you can go with the flow and let life do the rest
You're taking a risk when you roll the dice
You win some, you lose some, that's just life
If you're lucky you might get to roll twice
If you don't, unlucky, but there's no need to fight
Because fighting never seems to solve much
Only pain is achieved from a violent touch
What can be changed by throwing a punch?
Not a lot will change or at least not enough
Forget the bad times and move on with the game
Look to the future without the pain
The future doesn't have to be the same
You were unlucky before but no one was to blame
Instead of stepping back, move forward a space
A game is to be enjoyed, if not it's a waste
Play in your style, not the latest craze
So when it's done you can say that you did it your way
When the game is over it has to end
Look back and reminisce on the good times and friends
The friends that helped you pass the game's test
And ask yourself, have you achieved success?
At the end it's sad, like saying goodbye
But were you a winner of 'the game of life'?

Julian Blankson (13)

Cruel Dreams

I dreamt of you last night
Of when you graced me with your presence
My heart wanders to my head
Why must we sleep when the sky turns dark?
Why must time rule our lives?
Why can't I blink
And instead turn back time . . .
To when we were naïve, and free to the world?
I wish we could have danced until the sun said stop
Why can't time stand still at these precious times
When I knew the real you?
Cruel dreams
When I first saw you, I felt like the
Wind had blown me in your direction
I think you stole my heart
And never gave it back
But imprinted on my soul for eternity
Must I grow old without your smile?
I am phased
But now our past is a blur
My eyes are smoke-screened
My lashes tingle, now my eyes are free
The sun pierces through the blinds
It's magical, but you're not near
A cruel dream made by desire
The desire to see you once more
Touch your face
And see that heart-warming smile
Such a dream
Such cruel dreams.

Rebecca Hollis (16)

Uncontrollable

So tired and unable
To speak my mind
But all the words I wanna say
Are simply whisked and washed away
Unto my life
I get to see
Flowing river washed to sea
Cars and bikes are seen free
All the world seems to be
Uncontrollable
A child seeks its mother
It cries and screams in grief
But all the words I wanna say
Are simply whisked and washed away
Unto my life
I get to see
Flowing river washed to sea
Cars and bikes are seen free
All the world seems to be
Is uncontrollable
A dolphin is in trouble
Its tail is in a net
But all the words I wanna say
Are simply whisked and washed away
Unto my life
I get to see
Flowing river washed to sea
Cars and bikes are seen free
Everybody seems to be
So uncontrollable.

Deanna Somers (14)

I Just Wanna Be Me (Mistaken Girl)

I am just a mistaken girl
I'm the odd one out in a different world
I'm the only one who'd do anything just to be free
Lots of girls wear these tarty clothes
And their parents buy them all, but who cares?
They earn loads
They all wanna be celebs, but I just wanna be me
That was
When I realised I was mistaken
And I am just a girl next door
And I wish I could be free
Right now
I could be all that I want
I could make myself a new promise
But I just wanna be me
I am not a wannabe *wag*
I don't give a damn if I'm in a gang
And who the hell came up with fitting in?
I just sit all day on my own
Leaving thoughts as thoughts, I won't say anymore
What's the point in insulting, when I just wanna be me?
That was
When I realised I was mistaken
I am just not all that special
I know I'll never be free
Right now
I could be all that I want
Though I know that it's impossible
Because I just wanna be me
And I just wanna be me.

Eleanor Grant (12)

I Can't Believe It

What can I do?
When my head is going through
Overload . . .
I'm running out of air
When I look
You stare . . .
Is it back at me?
It feels like being torn into pieces
Like not knowing where to run
So all I can do is sit here
Waiting
Waiting for you to come
I can't believe it
I can't see us with anyone else
It's harder than words can describe
I need you here tonight
I can't believe it
When I'm down you're always around
I can't believe that you're gone
I miss you so much
I wish you knew
That I love you
I can't believe it
I can't see us with anyone else
It's harder than words can describe
I need you here tonight
I can't believe it
I missed out my chance
I need you to know
That I love you so . . .

Abbie Squire (12)

Losing You

Hanging out at the park with the gang
We used to have such a laugh
With me and you it was deeper
We knew each other so well
With you I could be myself
I could tell you anything
You told me what your dad does to you
I could see the pain in your eyes
I hugged you so tight and I never let go
You told me not to tell anyone
We had been talking for hours
I told you I couldn't make that promise
When I came to call on you
Your parents would say that you weren't in
I know that you were there, I could see you in the window
You would stare at me, I would smile at you
Turn around and come back the next day
I was never going to give up on you
I sat you all down and I confronted him
Your mum started to cry, your dad started to lie
You ran to your room and I followed you
You had locked the door, so I kicked it down
Then I saw you hanging from your school tie
You were so pale and I just cried
When I look back on our relationship
I see all the good times, I block out all of the bad times
I want you to know that I was there for you
I want you to know that I cared about you
I want you to know I could never judge you
And I want you to know that I love you.

Oresiriteru Ikogho (14)

Our Number One Aim

I believe in a God who is totally fair,
Who looks at our hearts and does not care
What country we are in, nor the colour of our skin,
For He is perfect love and hates such sin.
In His world racism does not belong:
Any prejudice is totally wrong.
Please listen to what I say, as I pray,
That finally one day, racism will go away.
Anti-racism - the name of this song
And the evil will be gone, before too long,
Yes, you heard me right, it will be gone.
What good comes out of it? Absolutely none.
We're all the same colour, our species is one
In one fragile world orbiting the sun.
God made us all equal - our cultures and our gifts
Are things to be celebrated, not to cause rifts.
From Bolt to Obama, it doesn't matter who,
Doing well ain't linked to race: I know that this is true.
We've gotta tell others what needs to be done,
As a team, different people must unite as one,
To be an example to the next generation,
Telling them there's no room for discrimination.
We shouldn't be scared to tell 'em what we know;
We're overdue the time that racism must go.
So together let's unite, join the fight, show the light,
Day and night, to tell people what we know is right.
It is clear for us and for all to see,
That racism has no place in society,
In telling you this I have no shame,
Let's make abolishing racism our number one aim.

Tim Perry (17)

Imagine The Heartache

When I saw you first I knew you were something new,
You reminded me of someone but somehow I didn't know who.
Your eyes they shone like diamonds, I got enchanted by your smile,
You reached out and took my hand and a place in my heart,
And I didn't mind you staying there for a while.
Don't tell me that you don't really care,
Tell me that you're sorry like I'm unaware.
The things you said they often hurt,
Yet you left me to cry alone in the dirt.
Saying you need a friend, was it all a lie?
Transfixed by you, yet I didn't know why.
Was it the way you made me laugh, or the way you held me near?
You told me not to let go, to keep being strong,
But try harder next time because what you said was unclear.
Don't tell me that you don't really care,
Tell me you're sorry like I am unaware.
The things you said they often hurt,
Yet you left me to cry alone in the dirt.
There were times when you told me I put a smile on your face,
Yet one day you told me you have to go, you needed your own space.
I've never had a friend as special as you,
You said you would always be here for me,
When you said forever I hoped it was true.
You told me you didn't really care,
Told me sorry and life was unfair.
You had to go and we had to be apart,
You were my best friend from the start.
You were with me until the end,
Now I'm older my heart's started to mend,
One day I'll lose you completely, my imaginary friend.

Antonia Roberts (15)

Just Another Teenage Girl

Life's a mess, full of drama that makes you upset
No second chances, making you doing the regret
Your life is hell, but you just don't know why
What is wrong with people, God, the world?
Everything, from the stuff you get hurled
Back off, give me a chance, I'm just a teenage girl
I'm nobody, no celeb, no superstar
Heck, don't ya think I don't know I won't go far?
Life isn't right for me, a loser or a freak
I'm a dork, a minger, a freak
I ain't Barbie and you aren't Brad Pitt!
I'm not blonde and you actually think you're fit
Get out of my life and don't come back!
Here's your bag, start to pack
My heart's broken, but yours was never there
It's probably a good thing, all you do is swear
Don't you sing me a love song, don't you cry
In fact I'd love you loads if you would die
Brilliant, you're leaving, oh my God, you're gone
Help, I'm dreaming, I'm rid of the one
Only it's just a dream
'Cause it's the real world
And I'm just
And I'm just
And I'm just . . . another teenage girl
Girl, girl, girl
Just another teenage girl
Girl, girl, girl
Just another . . .
Teenage girl.

Ceri Richmond (14)

Demons

There might be demons,
Waving at you from the dance floor.
So don't just sit around,
You got to get up, get out, show them what you're all about.
Make yourself seen,
Make yourself heard, if it means you have to shout.
Don't get left behind,
You don't want to be the one hiding behind the crowd,
In the corner, not making the slightest sound.
Put yourself first,
Be noticed, else soon it will be a curse,
That they'll take advantage of the fact
That you're too afraid to fight back.
Don't let anyone invade your private space,
If they do, then out them, back to the correct place.
Don't let them think that they can walk all over you,
Make them feel as if they're losing a very fast race.
You know that some day
No matter how or why, things just seem to come your way.
But to get there,
You need to learn that life is more than one shade of grey,
That there'll be differences in every single friend you've made,
That life is not one big game you play.
Don't be a stranger,
Or you'll find yourself having one big price to pay.
You should realise,
That you'll still have demons coming up behind you,
Be aware and don't get taken by surprise,
In case they catch up with you,
Be ready so that if there's a battle, you won't lose.

Jessica Timlin (15)

Smiling Like A Fool

It all started with chemistry,
When I was seated next to you,
I never really knew you before,
But from then on, sparks flew.
You would annoy others,
With your childish behaviour,
And the tricks you had up your sleeve,
But I started to see you differently,
And I started to slowly warm up,
To your special cuteness.

One chemistry lesson,
We were looking at cells through a microscope.
As I sat down next to you,
You reached forward to look through,
And you caught me by surprise,
When our faces were only a breath apart.
With a slight turn of my head to the left,
My lips would have touched your cheek.
Like an arrow out of nowhere,
You hit the centre of my heart.

Chorus
Boy, whenever I see you now,
Every time I think of you,
You got me falling off my stool,
I end up smiling like a fool.
My heart would fly like fireworks,
My other thoughts subside,
Cos boy, you got me,
Smiling like a fool.

Pauline Ocampo (15)

The End

Verse
Turn the TV on
The pictures move, but in my head there's nothing on
There's no light, there's no sound
I just feel like (feel like) I'm falling down.

Chorus
The end is nearing now
I wish I could see the light for one last time
But after all this
I don't think I'll ever resurface.

Verse
The blackness is closing in
I think I'm just gonna let it win
Because death must be peaceful, safer
From the pain and lies in life.

Chorus
The end is nearing now
I wish I could see the light for one last time
But after all this
I don't think I'll ever resurface.

Extended chorus
Somebody help me!
What did I do wrong?
The pain is ceasing now, and I've stopped falling
Now I'm just drifting
I just wish somebody would catch me
And tell me that after all this . . .
I will resurface.

Bethany Ibberson (13)

Who Knew?

Remember when we were younger,
And we'd play all day?
Don't you wish you could go back
To those happy days
Where all the laughter filled our eyes with tears?
Sitting in the park watching the world, the world go by
And thinking why, oh why
Did I waste all this time?

I should have asked you at the time,
But I've only just realised,
That I want you to be mine,
I want you to hold me tight,
And tell me everything's going to be alright.

Well, I'm reaching out to you,
With everything I own,
Wishing you'll be the one
To walk me home at night
And kiss me goodbye.

Oh, I wish that you knew,
But I'm not brave enough to,
To tell you,
That when I close my eyes,
I only see you,
You're the only one that makes me smile
When I'm about to cry,
I need you more than you will ever know.

You just need to remember when we were younger
And I was next to you.

Caitlin Anderton (15)

Fun!

Teachers say there's no more fun
It's school now
work must be done

I think about when it was the holidays
havin' loads of fun
chillin', chattin', swimming, laughing
but good times have now done.

Teachers say there's no more fun
It's school now
work must be done

I fall asleep and dream 'bout fun
the carnival, shooting guns
on the rides stomach turns
but I'm really in school
... and it burns

Teachers say there's no more fun
It's school now
work must be done

My teacher Mr Pigions screams,
'Girl, get out of my class!'
I walk outside
then run and hide
Caretaker catches me,
'You're in trouble lass.'

Teachers say there's no more fun
It's school now
work must be done, done, done, done.

Georgina Greaves (12)

What Do You Make Me Do?

When I see your smile,
It lights up my day,
Even if it's been a while
Your voice just makes me wanna crumble and break apart . . .
When I am around you, I only mumble,
And the things you do, they seem so humble,
But honestly, with you I haven't got a clue of what to do.
Because . . .
You make me wonder,
You make me cry,
You make me wanna hold ya tight,
Even though I know you lie . . .
The way you touch me,
The way you speak,
Just brings me all the way down . . .

Cos I know your secret,
The way you look at her, as if she is a prize . . .
You know you won't win,
You know you can't win,
So why even try?
We have a life to begin.
Your deep brown eyes, they comfort me,
I almost forget the lies.
Some say that love is blind
And that you need that special sign,
But you gave me that sign
And I followed like a child crossing the road,
But I didn't have that hand to hold,
And now my heart has been sold!

Puneet Bhachu (14)

Hiding Myself

I can lie through my teeth
About just anything
I can get up and say
That I'm fine, I'm okay
But the truth is already gone
And the answers, already lost

Commence the questions
The interrogation
Pull down the boundaries and let it all loose
Hurting everyone with the painful truth
It's our choice to keep it locked away
Yet feel the sting of what others say
Or put on a fake smile
And let us all lie
While we battle the demons that rage inside

I convince myself I'm not good enough
And I hide behind the real me
When I look in the mirror
It's only stupid faults that I see
Because I lack faith to simply believe

Why do I keep trying
To pursue my dreams?
I can't catch these stars
They're not as close as they seem
Now I'm back to square one
Lying to you like before
And I'll fake another smile
Before my armour cracks once more.

Niamh White (12)

Gone For Good

Gone for good, gone for good
I thought you'd never leave me
Gone for good, I want you back
I hope that you believe me
Gone for good

As I stare into the distance
I think and wonder why
You've left me now forever
And didn't say goodbye

You've left me broken hearted
All numb and dead inside
I dreamt that you would be my husband
And I your loving bride

Gone for good, gone for good
I thought you'd never leave me
Gone for good, I want you back
I hope that you believe me
Gone for good

I never will forget you
You'll always be on my mind
You thought that I would move on
Yet you know I'm not that kind

Gone for good, gone for good
I thought you'd never leave me
Gone for good, I want you back
I hope that you believe me
Gone for good.

Gemma Nangle (13)

When I First Saw You

When I first saw you
I didn't think you liked me
I've never felt so hurt
But now I know, I was a fool

Chorus
'Cause I love you and you love me too
But it was too good to be true
There was a feeling deep inside
That made me want to hold you tight

It all started on a cloudy night
When you walked round the corner and into my sight
Then I saw your amazing smile
And I stared at you for a little while

When I came round to see how you were
That was when I first saw her
She was the girl with the golden hair
And you looked like the perfect pair

Chorus
'Cause I love you and I thought
You loved me too
But it was too good to be true
There was feeling deep inside
That made me want to hold you tight

Now I know that you betrayed me
And now it is clear to see
Now I can't even look your way
'Cause it brings back the hurt from that day.

Hannah Portsmouth (13)

Take 'Em Down

Feeling fine, feeling mean
Today's the day we meet that team
Travelling south, the music's loud
Gonna get those points, gonna come home proud.

The ice is cold, my head is hot
Warming up for a killer shot
Come on boys, let's take 'em down
Take 'em down, run 'em outta town.

Wind it up boys, high and hard
Drive it, force it, skate it, take it
Slap it, crash it, burn that ice
Gotta get between those pipes first time.

Goal for us, goal for them
Those boys were smoking, this game must end
Legs are burning, smiles are wide, we group together
Gonna take 'em down, they're outta bounds.

Scores are level, last line out
Grit your teeth boys, there ain't no doubt
A black tornado seals the deal, it ain't
Our hearts that've gotta heal
We took 'em down, they're outta sound.

We wound it up boys, worked 'em hard
Drove it, forced it, skated it, took it
Slapped it, crashed it, burned that ice
We owned that team, they lost the fight
Lost the fight, lost the fight
Lost the fight . . . (fade).

Cole Shudra (11)

Life Worthy

I don't know if you know me
I don't know if you care
I think you're so stubborn
in every way.
I feel so insecure
when you're with her
And I think you're obnoxious
All the time
Can't you see
Oh, can't you see
that you're not living
the real life?
You need to wake up, wake up
And live life to the full
Wake up, wake up
Don't sit and look like a fool
Maybe, maybe
If you looked around
You might need to put
your feet on the ground
Woah, woah
let's dance around
Woah, woah
to the beat of the sound
And maybe you'll find
You'll find
That life's worthy
yeah
all right.

Molly Wooders (13)

Hypocrisy Club

Welcome to the Hypocrisy Club,
Everyone's a member,
Hypocrisy Club,
Every age and gender,
Hypocrisy Club,
Please just remember,
Everybody here is a hypocrite.
I don't like hypocrites,
But I can't get away from the fact that
I am one too,
It's nothing new.
Hypocrisy Club,
Everyone's a member,
Hypocrisy Club,
Every age and gender,
Hypocrisy Club,
Please just remember,
Everybody here is a hypocrite.
You tell me to do this then you do that,
I tell you to do this then I do that,
You tell me to do this then you do that,
I tell you to do this then I do that.
Hypocrisy Club,
Everyone's a member,
Hypocrisy Club,
Every age and gender.
Hypocrisy Club,
Please just remember,
Everybody here is a hypocrite.

Gary Crackett (13)

Is This Real?

Are you really looking at me
Or are you just looking through?
What can you really see?
What I wouldn't give to be you.
I really hate the way you make me feel,
Roaming around is the best thing I got,
What could I do to make these wounds heal?
I could have done better,
You're the meanest of the lot,
So why do I still love you?
Will this feeling go away?
I just wish you loved me too,
But today's another day.
You're good at winding me up,
Can't you just see it?
The way I look you up and down,
But is this real, is it?
So why do I still love you?
Will this feeling just go away?
I just wish you loved me too,
But today's another day.
You cause me pain but I can't look away,
I love you too much can't you see?
Are you blind to me cause I'm not your type?
What I wouldn't give for you to love me,
So why do I still love you?
Will this feeling go away?
I just wished you loved me too,
But today's another day!

Corinne Smith (13)

Me And You

You're the one that I'll cherish and love
You're the angel that came from above
I'll be there to care for you
Day and night through and through
Come let me pull you out the rain
When I hold you close you'll feel no pain
We'll watch the sun pull across the sky
I can't believe it you are mine
Me and you have a special bond
So special it can reach the stars and beyond
You're my hopes, my dreams, my world
And I'm so proud to call you my girl
Me and you we'll stay together
Me and you we'll last forever
I wrote this song for us, the lovers
Taking a chance for one another
Right here is where I want to be
With me holding you
And you close to me
There's nothing I wouldn't do
To show you that I'm loyal and I'll stay true
Me and you tonight
This is gonna feel right
Me and you today
Buy you pearls on payday
Girl when we're together
Man, I feel better
We're gonna spend the rest of our days together
Because it's just me and you.

Connor Moorcroft (13)

Untitled

Let it all out, let it all out,
Come to me, talk to me,
Tell me why you have been so down lately.
I miss you, I miss you,
I miss your laugh, your smile,
You are something I'd never want to change.
You feel down,
You feel you're going to drown,
But let me tell you this,
That I am dying for your kiss.
You may feel like you are nothing,
But to me you are everything,
You are my sanctuary, my sanctuary,
But I need more affection than you know.
You are my only, my only one,
I know you don't think this about me,
But bottling it up inside,
Is killing me, I'm dying,
I'm trying to make you see,
What you mean to me.
Even if I lose myself, lose myself in you,
I shall continue to walk,
With you by my side,
That is something I never want to change
You may feel like you are nothing,
But to me you are everything,
You are my sanctuary, my sanctuary,
But I need more affection than you know,
I need more affection than you know . . .

Lauren Teasdale (15)

Girl In The Blue Dress

The black and white people oblivious
She floats by unseen
Her colour unreal and intense
Nowhere she'd rather be
Caught up in her imaginary world
Humming to herself in bliss
Closed off to humankind
The girl in the blue dress
Can you envision?
Can you suppose?
Put yourself in her clothes
And be her for the day
Can you imagine?
Can you believe?
What would she think
And what would she say?
Free to wander and free to pretend
The girl in the blue dress
The girl with no friends
The bustling streets whiz past
But she stays autonomous
Her own world wanders
At a slower pace to the rest
Slow and secluded
Ditched and deserted
Brushed aside
Burnt inside
The girl in the blue dress
The girl with no friends.

Esme MacKrill (15)

The Unknown Star

As he sat in the chair
outside the room
his heart was pounding
like the strike of noon.
His name was called
it was far too soon
his first audition
at The New Blue Moon.
He's the unknown star
singing from bar to bar
just singing his song
and strumming along.
He was chosen by a scout
what a chance in life
the atmosphere changed
you could cut it with a knife,
and after a pause
he finally said yes
he made the right decision
his life was a mess.
He's the unknown star
singing from bar to bar
just singing his song
and strumming along.
His name in lights
It's so different from the bar,
with screaming fans
and a stretch limo car
He's the *unknown star!*

Matthew Davis (12)

This Is A Dream

It started off at twelve
In the garden of angels
I looked in your eyes
You looked in my eyes
Could it be?
I've always wanted love in my life, yeah
Single is so lonely and dark
Having someone else is so much better
Please let me have a chance
I've always wanted to be on the other side
Love at first sight
After a week of love and magic
Friendliness and so much love
You took me somewhere peaceful
Then silence came above
You knelt on one knee
You said, 'Will you marry me?'
And our dream started there
I've always wanted love in my life, yeah
Single is so lonely and dark
Having someone else is so much better
Please let me have a chance
I've always wanted to be on the other side
Love at first sight
When that day dawned
Happiness and fear inside our heads
I walk down the aisle of dreams
Then I stare at you, hand in hand
This just seems like a dream!

Chloe Cannon (11)

Untitled

She trembles and they watch their breath,
Synchronised exhalations and a melancholy sigh
Flows between them, fleeter than their quick-step
Crystallizing in each other's eyelashes
Twined hands share the secret;
She whispers, he wavers, the infinitely reflected
Words that are not words, they bounce between
The eyes of illicit lovers, the secret unseen.
The first sparked the rapture, now nothing's enough,
And you can't teach a teenager to stay out of love.
Bursts through hot flesh, torn open white dress,
Her heart now raw rhythm-less meat
Left to congeal upon somebody else's shoes.
Remember his static dance, the children stood still?
They froze before, frightened away,
They dared only to tell him what all but he knew,
But he can't stand to see these two children at play.
The first sparked the rapture, now nothing's enough,
And you can't teach a teenager to stay out of love.
Silk tickles trails across skin, twisted from lies,
With blooms like ivy, ruptured shivering veins,
Spiderweb carpets over innocent skies,
Watching them swiftly lose theirs;
It's so much simpler from this high up,
Where light binds the invasive, intrusive black stares.
Struggling to crawl deeper into their mess, they've been
Saved by the knowledge that they cannot be seen.
Their breath warms only themselves, and he remains screaming
Too young for his obscure songs to be granted their meaning.

Eleanor Equizi (15)

131

Friends Forever!

You and me are opposites
Until one day we found each other.
Our lives have just started
Will I know you through all of it?
So please tell me,
Are we friends forever
or are we just good friends for now?
Do you like me better
than those teenage jerks down there?
People call us sisters
cause we're always together,
So tell me Leah
'Cause I need to know.
We met last year
I thought I'd never have a chance
to be your friend, never mind best friends.
We make each other laugh.
We make each other cry.
But what I need to know is,
Are we friends forever
or are we just good friends for now?
Do you like me better
than those teenage jerks down there?
People call us sisters
cause we're always together.
So tell me Leah
'Cause I need to know,
'Cause I need to know,
'Cause I need to know.

Leonie Farrar (12)

Untitled

I've listened to your message tone
A thousand times
And I can recognise your voice
Line by line
Underneath it all even you can't find
That you've been hiding for years
So, tell my boy
What you're thinking
In your mind
Is it reason?
You're like pen to paper
Fire to fly
Always playing
Can't find rewind
You're a dreamer not a thinker
There's so much you can do
But your heart's locked together
With sticky tape and glue
You put on a front to me
And your friends
But what will you do when
Your game ends?
You can shut your eyes
And pretend not to see
What you've been hiding for years
Do what they tell you
Follow the carving on the tree
Get the scissors out
Let your heart be free.

Jessica Girdwood (15)

Dream

Way above the sky
a life that's all yours
dream a big dream
where people are all different
in a world of memories
dream a big dream
in which people do everything
in a peaceful world
you can dream a big dream
your heart can be empty
or your heart can be filled with love
but in this dream of happiness
it's all about the world above
so dream a big dream
with a smile and a tear
just focus on what's going on
all the way up here
close your eyes and think about
everyone you love
tell them how much you need them
in this world above
dream a big dream
don't let people stop you
dream a big dream
you never know they might come true
run, fly and reach out
that's what you need to do
dream a big dream
and I'll be there for you.

April Spencer (15)

Flying Too Close To The Sun

We would soar to the heavens,
We were flying that high,
We'd dance on delicate clouds,
Underneath a dawning sky.
In the day we'd fly over deep oceans,
Our hands dipping in sunlit sea,
It was so much fun, just gliding along,
Yeah, it was perfect when it was you and me.
When it got dark, we'd reach for the stars,
And picnic on the moon.
Our eyes locked, our hands entwined,
Why'd it end so soon?
'Cause now we're falling into deep waters,
'Cause we were flying too close to the sun.
I'm struggling to breathe, I'm begging you please,
Can you hear me anyone?
I felt you fallin' beneath me,
Just a little, inch by inch.
When we flew to the brightest star,
You couldn't get there, you couldn't reach.
We must have been staring into each other's eyes,
So we didn't notice when the sun melted our love disguise.
We must have not noticed when our feathers fell apart
And drifted below,
Falling to a tumbling waterfall,
Then into the sea's flow . . .
Good things don't last . . .
Hold onto what you have . . .
Don't fly too close to the sun.

Áine Maher (12)

Undone

I've got something to say,
Let me put it this way,
You brighten my day
When you're here by my side,
I can't stop smiling,
But I can't forget you lied,
You held my hand,
Took a stand,
Told me you'd never let me go . . .
I've got to run away from everything,
Get away from you,
I thought you were the one
And it was fun,
But after it all, how did we become so undone?
Maybe it's a good thing we moved on,
I've got loads of new friends,
It didn't take me long,
I've still got the memories,
But I'll replace them,
Cos me and you were way back then,
You held my hand,
But I took a stand,
I told you its time to let me go . . .
I've got to run away from everything,
Get away from you,
I thought you were the one,
And it was fun,
But after all we went through,
It's a good thing we became undone.

Amy Greatrex (13)

Look At Me

Look at me, not at her,
What is it that she does for you?
I am here, but so is she,
Why can't you see?
She's your girlfriend, but I'm your best friend,
Shouldn't I know better?
Cos I've known you, all my life,
And now it's time to say,
It's not too late, it never was,
But very soon it might be,
Cos she's caught you, in her web,
Why won't you break free?
And look at me, not at her,
What is it that she does for you?
I am here, but so is she,
Why can't you see,
And come running back to me?
Questions, I have many,
But what I need to know,
Is when you've heard, heard everything,
And you know it all,
Will you love me, like you should,
Or will you turn away from,
Will you turn away from what we have?
So look at me, not at her,
What is it that she does for you?
I am here, but so is she,
Why can't you see,
And come running back to me?

Emma Bradley (16)

The Promise

He was just a lil' boy
In a great big world.
His daddy held him tight and said,
'Listen to me, son, take care of your mum
I'm going away, but I won't be long'
The lil' boy cried,
'Promise to be home for my birthday,
It's in 365 days'
He cried with his mum as his daddy left
In a green van and a rifle in hand.
He was just a lil' boy, in a great big world.
His daddy held him tight and said,
'Listen to me, son, take care of your mum,
I'm going away, but I won't be long.'
It was almost his birthday,
Twelve more days to go, but late that night,
His mummy came in, took him in her arms
And cried, 'I'm so sorry, son, your daddy won't be back
In time for your birthday. He won't be back soon,
I know he misses you.
Your daddy said his final goodbye before he died
And he promises to see you later in time.'
He was just a lil' boy
In a great big world,
His best friend is gone,
But he has to stand strong
And keep his promise to care for his mum.
He was just a lil' boy
Alone in the big world.

Christina Rogers (14)

Two Different Points Of View

When I frown,
My eyes do too.
They scream the words, *I miss you.*
Love is a strong word,
And I thought you cared.
But now my broken heart's
Left to be repaired.
You covered it in gasoline
And now it's set alight.
My heart's replaced with a burning hole
Which you've left me here, to fight . . .

When you smile,
Your eyes do too.
They scream the words, *I love you.*
The moonlight dances in your midnight eyes.
Every word you say
With your beautiful voice,
I memorise.
I wish I could protect your heart
So that my cruel words won't tear you apart.
'You're too good for me
Someday you will see.'

I've struck the match.
Your heart's been lit.
I didn't want to be the guy to have to do it.
But it's the best thing for you that I could do.
This is why we're different,
Two different points of view.

Hannah Davies (14)

Right Beside You

I've had this feeling for so long
Inside of me, pulling me down
but I'm still holdin' strong
I'm still going on.
And I don't know what to do,
I don't know how I'll make it through
how to make it through
If it wasn't for you
right there
right beside me, yeah.

When you're around
I can't help but stare
And for some reason I always
see you everywhere
You were always there right beside me
When you smile I smile too
When you look at me I look at you
And when I look into your eyes
there's always a surprise
It's like fireworks in the sky
Shining down on us.

Everything is clear, when you're near
This is what we're meant to do
'Cause I need to be next to you
I need to have your heart next to me for all time
I need to know when you're near
Because I love you sooo much my dear
And I need to be here, (right next to you).

Philamena Holden (12)

Breaking My Heart

I look into your eyes
I see the puddles of blue
I look into your heart
I write a message just for you
I look into your soul
You're as happy as can be
I look into your dreams
And see you with someone that isn't me

Breaking my heart seems easy for you
And I hope one day
Someone will do it to you too
And then you'll know how bad it feels
When someone has broken, broken your heart

You look into my eyes
You see the way I feel
You look into my heart
And see that this is real
You look on the ground
Not knowing what to say
I look into your mind
It's the only way, the only way I know

Breaking my heart seems easy for you
And I hope one day
Someone will do it to you too
And then you'll know how bad it feels
When someone has broken, broken your heart
Broken your heart, broken your heart.

Siân Loveland (13)

Miss Dolly Daydream

Miss Dolly Daydream
You're the sitcom writer's muse
The one with broken dreams
When you wake up
You hear those screams
Of memories from once upon a time

Sixteen years of anything but innocence
Becoming the childhood sweetheart
The big heart breaker
Of a thousand boys

One day little boy blue came along
Big wide eyes
Was he some sort of perfection
Or was it just plain lies
Wrapped up inside your idea of paradise?

He hit you hard
And you fell down, down, down
Until you hit the floor
You're not the childhood sweetheart anymore

I'm Miss Dolly Daydream
I wear ripped, skinny jeans
And the cardigan of my long lost lover
I'm not takin' it off
Not ever

Maybe I should let go
I just can't let go.

Abigail Sutton (16)

Be Free With Me

From tomorrow comes today,
And yet you're still so far away,
Tied by chains of 'eventually'
When will it be just you and me?

Welcome to reality
Till chains are cut you're never free
Believe me, now the time is right
For you to love, to live your life.

Make the jump, take the risk
Find out what freedom really is
Take my hand, let music play.

Let the moonlight be your spotlight
And the audience the stars
Now is your chance to show them
Who you really are.

Fill the world with laughter
Make every step a dance
Smile and just be happy
Now is your only chance.

Be free with me
Be free with me
Feel the wind upon your face
Cast chains aside, don't look back
For life is love and love is free
Be free with me
Be free with me.

Adam Dyster (15)

Looking For You

I've been living with a shadow over my head
I've been sleeping with a cloud over my bed
I've been looking for someone to help me through
Looking for someone to hold my hand
I'm looking for you
Just waiting for you
Just watching for you
to help me through
Every day without you
is a burden for me
I can't think of anything new
Looking for someone to hold my hand
I'm looking for you
Just waiting for you
Just watching for you
to help me through
Days seem meek
Without you
It makes me weak
Without you
I'm looking for you
Just waiting for you
Just watching for you
to help me through
I've been living with a shadow over my head
I've been sleeping with a cloud over my bed
I've been looking for someone to help me through
Looking for someone to hold my hand.

Christopher Naughton (13)

Last Time

Last time I let you in
You didn't leave
This time I lock the door
And throw away the key
Last time you built me up
You knocked me right back down
This time I stay afloat
And it's your turn to drown
I turned my back and left
Without one single regret
And I still have time to forget
Your words cut me like knives
Every single time
Now we can get on with our lives
Last time you lied to me
I believed everything
This time I'm the one
To hurt you with my sting
Last time you said you'd catch me
You let me fall
This time I'll run away
And not care at all
I turned my back and left
Without one single regret
And I still have time to forget
Your words cut me like knives
Every single time
Now we can get on with our lives.

Alice Baker (13)

The Vengeance Stage

With this kiss of death
With this kiss of death
With my last breath
I'ma take you down
With these evil eyes
With these evil eyes
hidden in disguise
I'ma take you down
You changed me
You made me
What I am today
You hurt me
deserted me
and now you will pay
With these venom lips
poisonous fingertips
let's take a trip
so I can take you down
Please don't fight back
don't try to attack
cause this is all just a trap
So I can take you down
You changed me
You made me
what I am today
You hurt me
deserted me
and now you will pay.

Rebeccah V Arthurs (15)

Spurring You On!

You want to be thin,
By throwing out that fatty food into the bin.
Think about those size 12 jeans,
Getting into them by ways and means.
You've got much slimmer,
Just by cutting down a little dinner.
So just think a few more stone,
But you gotta know you're never alone.
Try hard and all those pounds will drop,
Before you pick up that Mars bar, *stop!*
You can achieve inside if you just see,
The outer person you want to be.
To spur you on I will be here,
Even giving you a lil' cheer.
Don't you see, you will look like a star,
Just carry on, but not too far.
You need to think, to join that smile,
You will now need your very own style.
But make sure you take a break,
Learning to be the one to give and *take!*
So before you say, 'I can't get there,'
Go on, just think about your figure, care.
You will be happy with your new frame,
You won't need to say I feel so ashamed.
Be able to be the person you want to be,
Stop and say that's going to be me.
Maybe one day you will be a good runner,
But also I know you're one hell of a stunner.

Kathryn Beaumont (14)

I Don't Care (Or Do I?)

I'm sitting in the dark
Don't know which way to go
Surrounded by my family
But some don't want to know.
I'm feeling sad and lonely
of being on my own.
Why won't they ever talk to me
Or even pick up the phone?
They don't even seem interested
Of what I am doing now
Can't understand why they don't care
Cos all we do is row!
I'm happy with the family I have
My mum and sister too!
A reunion is out of the question
As it's too long overdue.
They love their own family
That's all I need to say.
Cos the family I see all the time
I think about every day!
They can stay away for all I care
I don't want to think about it
I have a boyfriend to look after me
And I do not care one bit!
I'm here for those who love me
When all is said and done
If you come anywhere near to me
I'll swear that I will run!

Naomi Williams (16)

Untitled

Wander along an unknown path
The wind plays tunes with the grass
Whispering softly I hear it sing
Calming enough to stop the sting.
My life is raining
I'm not complaining
Struggling to see
Sometimes wish I wasn't me
Eyes drenched with sorrow
Look to tomorrow
But there's no helping hand
Feel like I'm drowning on land
As the river flows
That's where my mind goes
As I try to put away
All the bad past of today
My mind becomes unlocked
Everything's no longer blocked
My life is raining
I'm not complaining
Struggling to see
Sometimes wish I wasn't me
Eyes drenched with sorrow
Look to tomorrow
But there's no helping hand
Feel like I'm drowning on land
No there's no helping hand
I'm alone where I stand.

Hannah Baker (15)

Smile On My Face

Words can't explain how I'm feeling
Cos I have you and a grin on my face
When you left my happiness you were stealing
But I'm taking you back with good grace.
And words can't explain how I'm feeling
You're so divine it just can't be true,
And the only time, I'm feeling fine,
Is when I'm right next to you!
I listen to you like a good girl,
When you tell me to keep off the streets,
You're the oyster, and I am your pearl,
In a film, where boy and girl meet!
Cos words can't express how I'm feeling,
When I have you and a grin on my face,
When you left, my happiness you were stealing,
But I've taken you back with good grace.
And everytime I try to run for cover
And break my chains and run free,
Think of a new life baby,
How may it be?
Without you, I trip and then I fall
Your love held tight in my hand,
I could never love any other
And, that's all – and
Words can't explain how I'm feeling
With youuuu, and a grin –
on – my – face!
I feel fine, cos you're mine!

Genevieve Tomes (12)

My Last Goodbye

Looking back down this winding road,
with only you in my sight
I see the depth of your betrayal
and the girl, standing on your right.
She looks at me
her mocking look quite plain
I know that you loved me once
but that won't ease the pain.
One step forward
a tear runs down my face
I'll never see you again
because she's taken my place.
I see the path before me
a long way I know
but I will travel forwards
through autumn's rain or winter's snow.
I turn to face you
and swallow my tears with pride
I know I can beat you
take it in one stride.
I have no more to say
I will win this war
I know I can someday
you're everything I once lived for.
But wait, there's one thing left to say
and although it breaks my heart
but this is my last goodbye
it's my chance for a fresh start.

Helen Lane (17) & Jennifer Lane (15)

Patchwork

'Where's my smile?' I heard you say,
'Come on, just for me.'
I stopped what I was doing, turned,
Turned so you could see,
My blue eyes burned with anger,
From words I couldn't say
And on my cheek, a ghastly mark,
Purple, blue and grey.
I hadn't tried to hide it,
I didn't think to care,
Because even if it's covered,
We know that it's still there.
The arguments at night-time,
Those I can't forget,
I'd raise my voice; you'd raise your fist,
Do you even regret?
This anger wells inside me,
But I can only cry,
Because if I try to oppose you,
I'll hurt another eye.
I live as a caged sparrow,
And soon I'll fly away
To somewhere where for once I'm loved
And I'm nobody's prey.
I'm waiting for my rapture,
My wait will be worthwhile,
But till that day when I am free,
Instead, I sigh and smile.

Antonia Qualey (15)

A Traveller's Dream

Lonely traveller on a broken road,
Pretty angel lets her wings unfold,
Lost and frightened got nowhere called home,
Wanders softly out there on her own,
And by chance if they should meet,
Should a romance be complete?
He could mend your wings,
He would ask you to dance right there,
Swing you round and round there's no need to be scared,
She could move your soul,
She could fix those broken dreams,
Fly you straight through the night,
Nothing's ever what it seems,
In a traveller's dream,
Round the corner is another world,
One step further you could meet this girl,
Turns direction takes a different view,
She'll sit there waiting till his journey's through,
And by chance if they should meet,
Should a romance be complete?
He could mend your wings,
He would ask you to dance right there,
Swing you round and round there's no need to be scared,
She could move your soul,
She could fix those broken dreams,
Fly you straight through the night,
Nothings ever what it seems,
In a traveller's dream.

Francesca Hayward (15)

153

Who's That Girl?

I stare at the wall
Feeling broken and small
Alone forever
Found someone never
Who's that girl?
Unwanted.
Why am I different?
Why can't I fit in?
Do my friends really like me?
Will I ever win?
Who's that girl?
Missing.
Why would anyone love me?
Perhaps I'm just strange
Sometimes I'd give anything
If it meant I could change
Who's that girl?
Forgotten.
I used to be happy
To be able to smile
Now each day I love
Feels like a trial.
Who's that girl?
Lost
If I tried to be different
Perhaps they would see.
How can I be special
When I'm stuck being me?

Amy Jackson (15)

Come Into My World

Life taught me to love nothing
I was so unimpressed and unreachable, but
The joys in your face renewed all my hopes
Your beauty was unspeakable, won't you ...
Break down the walls,
Force yourself in,
That's what it takes,
For dreams to begin.
I'm fragile and lost,
I'm scared and alone,
All I want is to know that
I am not on my own.
Why am I still, waiting on you?
Why aren't you yet by my side?
You're all that I have, all that I love,
Blow the door to my soul open wide.
Break down the doors,
Force yourself in,
That's what it takes
For dreams to begin.
I'm fragile and lost,
I'm scared and alone,
All I want is to know that
I am not on my own.
Come into my world and make sense of it,
There's too many lights and white noise,
The world's a stranger; I'm no part of it.
It only takes, withers and destroys.

Hannah Roe (18)

It Gets Me Through

I don't know what you do that gets me through,
It keeps me going, all because of you.
You seem to pick me up when I am down,
and I feel so alone, when you're not around.
Because with you, my tears slowly fade away,
and I miss you when you are gone and I really gotta say,
That I love you and I know that this is true.
Coz you're the only thing that gets me through.
I can't bear the thought of leaving you behind,
I mean come on, seriously.
You're always on my mind.
I don't want to imagine a life without you,
I think it would suck.
I really really do!
Because with you my tears slowly fade away,
and I miss you when you are gone and I really gotta say,
That I love you and I know that this is true.
Because you're the only thing that gets me through!
I don't know what you do that gets me through
It keeps me going all because of you
You seem to pick me up when I am down,
and I feel so alone, when you're not around.
Because with you my tears slowly fade away!
And I miss you when you are gone and I really gotta say!
That I love you and I know that this is true!
Because you're the only thing that gets me through
Yeah!
You're the only thing that gets me through!

Stewart Wivell (14)

You

You . . .
You take my breath away.
In the dark of night
I see you shine so bright,
So bright I see like it was day.
In the dead of night I burn
And I feel like I could die.
Your mind I cannot turn
And my heart and soul they cry.

You . . .
You're burning me inside
And I know you're his,
Give him your warmth, your kiss,
When he's with you my eyes I hide.
In the dead of night I burn
And I feel like I could die.
Your mind I cannot turn
And my heart and soul they cry.

You . . .
You don't see him no more.
But my luck's unchanged
You still turn me down the same
Crying at night just like before.
In the dead of night I burn
And I feel like I could die.
Your mind I cannot turn
And my heart and soul they cry.

James McMahon (17)

You And Me

You and me together
You and me forever
You make me laugh
You make me smile
You make my days all worthwhile
You and me
Never gonna be

You with me
Or against me
You with me
I hope
You against me
I know

You and her away
You and her today
You and me
Never gonna be
Together

You with me
Or against me
You with me
I hope
You against me
I know

You and me never gonna be
Together.

Danielle Hudson (12)

Why Did You Leave Me?

You have been there for me
Made me so glad
Now you have left me
And I'm feeling sad
Why did you leave me?
Oh why did you leave?

You came then you left
Why did you go?
Now I'm so lonely
I'm on my own
Why . . . oh why did you leave me?

I'll be crying forever
Who do you think you are?
This time for certain
You've gone way too far
Why did you leave me
Oh why did you leave?

I wish I was fine now,
To say, 'Just go away'
Cos I'm kinda tired
Of feeling this way
So why did you leave me?
I just want to know.

You came then you left
The question is
Why . . . oh why . . . oh why?

Zoe Paes (12)

Let's Not Play Again

Is this the game you're playing?
Because I don't feel like playing too.
It's not fair the way you get control
And I am forced to play along.

Please make it stop, I'm paralysed under you,
I keep falling deeper and I know my thoughts are true.
Please make it stop, I'm screaming with the pain,
I'm locked under your force, let's not play again.

You draw me so close to winning,
Then send me back to the start.
I feel I want to drop out forever,
But you hold me in too deep.

Please make it stop, I'm paralysed under you,
I keep falling deeper and I know my thoughts are true.
Please make it stop, I'm screaming with the pain,
I'm locked under your force, let's not play again.

'Cause I don't want this to hurt anymore,
It burns straight through my skin,
Crawling deeper into my heart,
I realise I'll never win.

Please make it stop, I'm paralysed under you,
I keep falling deeper and I know my thoughts are true.
Please make it stop, I'm screaming with the pain,
I'm locked under your force, let's not play again.

No, let's not play again.

Sharna Cottey (14)

Ruby

She's funny and lively
Cuddly and cute
Silly and adorable
That's Ruby

Fluffy and bouncy
Obedient and clever
She brightens my day
I'll love her forever

She's funny and lively
Cuddly and cute
Silly and adorable
That's Ruby

Energetic and wild
Active and fun
With a cute button nose
And as gold as the sun

She's funny and lively
Cuddly and cute
Silly and adorable
That's Ruby

Caring and devoted
Crazy as can be
Loyal and loveable
She's the one for me.

That's Ruby!

Grace Mangham (11)

Hold Me

Tell me how can I live without them?
How can I live without the ones I love most?
How can I say that I won't stay?
I wanna stay with you, hold you in my arms.
Trust in you like the old times.
Believe that you love me too and everything's alright.
But I can't! Yes I can!
Believe in them . . .
And I love you like my own child.
And never leave your side . . .
Cos I can never leave you!

Think about all the times
I've been there for you.
So stay with me and hold me in your arms.
Say that you love me and never let me go.
Cos how can I live without the ones I love most?
Well sometimes you have to hate the ones you love
Cos they are the only ones who can really hurt you.
But the only ones who can help you too.
So stay with me, hold me in your arms.
I trust you. Yes, I doooo.
I want to bring peace across the world
And I'm sure with your help I will do so.
Help me ban the hatred in this world
And stop people dying from hunger.
Me and you will save the world together,
So stay with me and . . . hold me in your arms.

Rachael Young (12)

Panoptic Design

You never veered from my horizon.
Constant in life's questioning equation,
And always controlling by panoptic design.
Your silence was gravitational,
Drawing the wolves to the prey,
The rats to the piper,
Yet we never bought Stockholm,
Until you showed us your syndrome.

With your red lipstick and cheap perfume,
Please go.
Heart-shaped necklaces and commanding small talk,
Please just let me go.
Release me from this magnetic flow.

You wear an angel's halo.
Underpinning those secret horns,
Ever illuminating those who obey,
An oasis of desire and danger.

Sensing cool electricity in the air,
I approached your bubbling potion.
Enticed by the colour of your scent,
Only to stumble on your rose-tinted lies.
So please, just let me go.
Release me from this magnetic flow.
Another nameless face,
With magazine smile, plastic heart . . .
And mannequin charm.

David Taylorson (17)

Driving In My Dressing Gown

(For Lucy)

Well, I set off one day
I was feeling quite dandy,
Felt like a trip
To some place rather sandy.
So I jumped in my car,
Not to go very far
And headed up the A428.

And I was driving in my dressing gown
Seeing what was occurring,
Driving in my dressing gown,
No one can stop me now.

So I carried on for a while,
Radio songs made me smile,
While the sun and the rain made a rainbow.
I thought of the east
And that my boyfriend's a beast
And maybe my attire's a little revealing.

So I was driving in my dressing gown,
Seeing what was occurring,
Driving in my dressing gown,
No one can stop me now.
Driving
In my dressing gown,
Driving
Out of town . . .

Briony Butterworth (14)

When The Small World Looks Too Big

You feel alone
Wrapping your arms around yourself
Sitting in a distant corner, the grim of the darkness stalking you, and
You feel alone
You feel alone

I'm trying, trying to get through
But it doesn't matter what I do
No, it doesn't matter what I say to you
You'll never know how much I love you

You're fading away now
Running from the world that made you feel this sorrow
You're drifting off now
Becoming impenetrable to even the people who truly care

Your heart feels like stone
And you want to cry every second of the day
But you don't want people to think you moan
So you keep falling away

I'm trying, trying to get through
But it doesn't matter what I do
No, it doesn't matter what I say to you
You'll never know how much I love you

You're fading away now
Running from the world that made you feel this sorrow
You're drifting off now
Ending in a bubble isolated from people around you.

Namrita Khosla (18)

I'll See You In Heaven

I still remember the times we had together
Oh how I wish you were here forever
Long walks across the sand, hand in hand
I think about you day and night
Standing at your death bed
I remember that last words you said
'I'll see you in Heaven'
I'll see you in Heaven, see you in Heaven
I cry myself to sleep at night
hoping things will turn out alright
I'll see you in Heaven
Sometimes I blink and see your face
then my heart beats to race
but when I blink again you're gone
I dream about me and you, what can I do?
Standing at your death bed
I remember the last words you said
'I'll see you in Heaven'
I'll see you in Heaven, see you in Heaven
I cry myself to sleep at night
hoping things will turn out right
I'll see you in Heaven
Oh I'll see you in Heaven
Standing at your death bed
I remember the last words you said
you said, 'I'll see you in Heaven'
I'll see you in Heaven.

Victoria Youster (12)

Together Forever

First day at school, new girl in town,
I look around me and then look down.
'Cause I see you stood over there,
Lookin' at me, hand through your hair.
And I know,
That you and me, we are meant to be,
Together forever for eternity.
That you and me, we are meant to be,
Together forever for eternity.
Our first date, it went as planned,
We walked and talked as you held my hand,
Time just flew right on by,
As I laughed with you and a tear in my eye,
'Cause I know,
That you and me, we are meant to be,
Together forever for eternity.
I know that you and me, we are meant to be,
Together forever for eternity.
Three years have passed since that day,
And we're still doin' fine,
'Cause you see from that very first moment,
I knew you'd still be mine.
'Cause I know,
That you and me, we are meant to be,
Together forever for eternity.
I know that you and me, we are meant to be,
Together forever for eternity.

Georgina Gleave (13)

Inside My Heart

All anyone ever wants is someone who cares
But the ones you love,
They don't even known when you're there
No one can make the same mistake, not twice, oh
If you love is as true as what you say
Your heart will lead you the right way.
They say it's not right, you're not nice, and I've gone so low,
But they don't understand,
They just don't know
They can't see
What I feel inside my heart
They just don't know . . . what could be.
Us two together, you and me
Is what no one wants to see,
This world, this day
And I don't think loving you
Is ever gonna go away.
I said your name
Now every girl thinks I'm lame.
Everything I do,
Every time I see your face
It's like I'm runnin' in a never-ending race.
It's like I can't breathe,
I just can't help being so naïve,
When you look inside your heart,
You will find,
All that you would leave behind.

Jessica Li (13)

Party

He's got a deal
Hey hey
That he lives with you for the weekend
Eat your 'nanas and meat
Use your toilet suite
That's a deal, hey hey

They've got a deal, whoo hoooo
That they live with your wife
Talk about your life
Cut food with your knife

Let's stay the night
Party till light
Listen to music
Let's do this Mick
Drink WKD
Party hard till 3

He's got a deal, hey hey
That he takes your car
Not the Jaguar
To his work in Rhyl
And take some pills

Let's leave dis house
Quiet as a mouse
Come back late
Maybe half 8.

Liam Anderton (14)

Coming Out

Every day I sit in silence wondering what to say.
Trying again and again to keep my feelings at bay.
'Cause the bullies kept coming over and over
And I finally snapped and said,

'So what, I'm a boffin, words won't hurt me today,
You've lost tonight.
Guess what, I've got one over on you
And you're gonna be cryin' tonight,
Well alright, I won the fight,
I'm gonna hurt you tonight.'

When I snapped I broke out my shell,
No fear of you or anyone else,
'Cause I'm carefree now, no worries at all,
The table's turned,
Now you're in the dumps and I'm loving life.

And now I am your greatest fear
After all the hurt and suffering I faced,
I'm getting revenge, I shoved in your face
And then you started again, and I clearly said,

'So what, I'm a boffin, words won't hurt me today,
You've lost tonight.
Guess what, I've got one over on you
And you're gonna be cryin' tonight,
Well alright, I won the fight,
I'm gonna hurt you *tonight.'*

Sam Fenton (11)

I Wish

I wish, I wish today weren't Friday,
It always makes me feel so sad.
I wish, I wish, today weren't Friday,
The girl that I could have had.

I woke up this morning and no one was there,
I thought that my girl would be sitting right there.

Chorus
But now she's gone
And nobody's there to hear me cry
And nobody's there to watch me die,
Watching the sun go by,
Watching the sun go by.

I thought we would spend,
All our life together,
I thought we would spend,
Every second with each other.

Chorus
But now she's gone
And nobody's there to hear me cry
And nobody's there to watch me die,
Watching the sun go by,
Watching the sun go by and the birds all cry as she passes me,
As she passes me,
'Cause she's my girl,
'Cause she's my girl.

Joel Morris (13)

Moonlighting

Whenever I go to New York
There's a place I never see
Where Park Avenue meets 42nd Street
The deli on the corner
Red chairs and tablecloths
That's the place we always used to meet.

Somewhere in the city
There's a girl I used to know
She goes out every night on her own
She says she's only had a few
But she's stumbling down the avenue
Singing memories in the moonlight, all alone.

We lived together for a while
Man, she used to make me smile
But, there was one thing made me cry
She'd be putting on a dress
And I knew she'd come back a mess
The only thing I didn't know was why.

Instrumental

But you have to realise
That you can't always fix it all
And there's only so much you can catch them
When they fall
There's only so much you can catch them
When they fall.

Elizabeth Potter (17)

Beauty

Beautiful as nature
Raw as raw
So pretty and untouched

Beauty lies within something true
True is beauty
Beauty is true
Beauty lies within me and you.

Beautiful body
Pure as pure
Mysterious and well loved

Beauty lies within something true
True is beauty
Beauty is true
Beauty lies within me and you.

Beautiful talent
Rare as rare
Individual and undiscovered

Beauty lies within something true
True is beauty
Beauty is true
Beauty lies within me and you

All this beauty is so free
One day when you will see
Hopefully you will start believing with me.

Sophie Wlazlo (13)

Exposed

Everything you did,
Everything that's done,
Leaves me stuck in this moment,
I can't move on.

I can't tell you how it made me feel,
What it made me do,
I can't recognise myself,
Still can't talk to you.

Several months later
I'm still in this place,
Don't know where to turn,
Which way to face.

I just can't be happy for you,
For all you put me through,
You left us all behind,
There's nothing I could do.

I look in the mirror,
I'm so ashamed,
You can't save me,
Or the person I became.

I'm too exposed,
I don't know how to go on,
You were my help,
But now you're gone.

Aislinn Baird (17)

Always There For You

I'm always there for you
When you're feeling blue
And then you fade away
I always try to stay
I'm always there for you!

Sonya Naoumoff (12)

Nothing's Really Changed

It's at times like this you're in my head
That make me think of all you said
And how you can't look in my eye,
But drift away and just pass by.

And in the silence you call me,
Although you just can't really see,
Nothing's really changed here,
Nothing's really changed.

And yes, the storms are here again,
I wonder, this time I'll call you friend?
Yeah, I don't feel we have re-engaged,
But then nothing's really changed.

It felt it would be better when
I said I loved you in that letter
The one I wish I never wrote
Cos you threw me back an empty note.

So tell me what you think I feel
When I see you with that other girl,
Holding hands the way we did,
It's like I'm a helpless lil' kid.

But after all you cannot see,
What you still mean to me
And still nothing's really changed
Nothing's really changed.

Serena Reeves (15)

Ray By Ray

So sing this song and say goodnight,
Then you can dream away,
Let your mind soar in flight,
You can awake from the light ray by ray.

Alyson Watson (13)

All I Believed

I hear the birds, I hear the bombs
People on the streets singin' old songs
The air, infested with pollution
Ain't no dreamers anymore to think up a solution

'Cause all I knew and all I believed
Has been crushed down
Like an old man's been deceived
God, you're so hard to believe
No angel's song is gonna help me find inner peace

Day turns to night
But all we change is truth into lies
Screams heard from miles away
Ain't heard at all unless we say

'Cause all I knew and all I believed
Has been crushed down
Like an old man's been deceived
God, you're so hard to believe
No angel's song is gonna help me find inner peace

Is it so hard to share? Care? Feel?

'Cause all I knew and all I believed
Has been crushed down
Like an old man's been deceived
God, you're so hard to believe
No angel's song is gonna help me find inner peace.

Jessica Frew (13)

I Don't Know

I have a feeling in my head,
I don't know what's
Gonna happen tomorrow,
What's gonna happen in the future?
What's happened in the past?
I don't know,
I don't know,
I don't know,
I doooon't know.
Will it shine?
Will it rain and pour?
Oh, I don't know.
Dinosaurs, were they real?
Robots, will they be true?
I can't tell you, but . . .
I don't know,
I don't know,
I don't know,
I doooon't know.
Will it shine?
Will it rain and pour?
Oh, I don't know.
What will happen to the Earth?
Will the trees be left to die?
I can't tell you but . . .
I don't know.

Scott Dallow (13)

Whisper Of Air

I never thought I could be this broken,
I never thought I'd want to fade away
And I woke from a dream without you here,
I woke from a dream to a world of tears,
And when the world burns out and you're still gone,
I just want to feel like I belong.
You're not there,
You're just a whisper of air,
When the stars come down
And fall to the ground,
I can't breathe without you here,
I can't live with you my dear,
I could hear your voice as I was fading out,
It pulled me back from a world of doubt,
As your words sang out don't fall towards the light,
But I fell into a world of night,
Where it's always dark and there's no warmth,
And I want you back with my everything,
I need you back without you I'm nothing,
I'm broken, I'm dreaming,
I want you home,
I'm broken, I'm dreaming,
I'm all alone,
And you're not there,
You're just a whisper,
A beautiful ghost.

Matthew Poynton (17)

The Young In Our Town

In this town we get abused, it's cos we're young,
We get used.
Some say we do wrong,
But all we do is have some fun!
Hanging round the town,
People always get us down.
We don't drink, we don't deal,
Like they say!
We are sensible, keep out of things
And enjoy our freedom and friends!
If we hang round in a gang, that's when they fear,
But all we're doin' is meeting mates,
Then we go off.
That's all we do, we're not dangerous.
We don't show our faces,
The oldies think we offend,
But at the base of it,
Hoodies are only fashion.
Hangin' round the parks we do no harm,
When it gets dark.
We stay out at night,
But don't get into fights.
I wish the older generation
Would give us some respect.
We do no harm,
We just meet mates and have fun.

Jasmine Gandy (13)

Alone

I stood there,
Looking for anyone,
Stood there all night,
not a person in sight.
I tried to call your name,
No one would come,
I truly felt alone,
Shivered to the bone.
Oh, I, I need you here right now,
Oh here, to heal the pain I feel,
Oh now, right now it's getting unbearable,
Oh I need you so I'm not alone.
I'm starting to lose it,
I'm not now in control,
It's tearing me apart,
I just want to depart,
I tried not to be alone,
But it just didn't work.
What can I do
without someone by my side?
Oh I, I need you here right now,
Oh here, to heal the pain I feel,
Oh now, right now it's getting unbearable,
Oh I need you so I'm not alone.
Alone, alone, alone, alone.
I need you.

Ross Templeman (13)

Let Me Out

The doors are closed and there's nowhere for me to breathe easy
Where do I hide, where do I go?
There's no step ladder or anything that shows no no
And I'm sitting here in the darkness of the night, ohhhhh yeah
And I'm waiting here in the early hours of dawn, yeah lalalala
Even if I have to write you a letter with a million words in it
And I cry at night thinking of tomorrow's ending, yeah, yeah
Am I gonna die or even see daylight?
These are my feelings, so can you let me out of the box now yeah?
These are my feelings, so can you let me out of the box now?
I feel like I'm strapped, in an endless world,
I can't breathe easy anymore, without you
And I cry, every tear for you
Every path I choose
I'm choosing it for you
Why can't you understand and let me out
Let me out
And I'm sitting here in the darkness of the night, ohhhhh yeah
And I'm waiting here in the early hours of dawn, yeah lalala
Even if I have to write you a letter with a million words in it
And I cry at night thinking about tomorrow's ending, yeah, yeah
Am I gonna die, or even see daylight?
These are my feelings, so can you let me out of the box now? Yeah
These are the feeling, so you need to understand
You need to let me out
Let me out.

Amy Proctor (12)

I Love You

You are the reason why I stand here today
You are the reason you brighten up my day
You are the reason why I feel whole
You make my life feel good
If only you knew how much you mean to me
If only I can find the words to say
I'm trying to say
How much you mean to me
I'm so lucky to be blessed with someone like you
To have someone who can pick me up when I am down
When I see you
My life turns right around
If only you knew how much you mean to me
If only I can find words to say
I'm trying to say
How much you mean to me
I need to
I need to
I need to find the words to say
I need you
I need you
So I can show you how much you mean to me
If only you knew how much you mean to me
If only I can find the words to say
I'm trying to say
I love you.

Alex Shaw (15)

Day To Day Basis

Some kids on a day to day basis
Get picked on because something's wrong with their faces
Or because they came from all different places
Problem is, he can't be protected
But it will get worse if the bullies are detected
The boy got so annoyed he's had enough
Got a kitchen knife, got all of his stuff
He knows, he knows where the boys hang
Plus he can hear them shouting and talkin' slang
He sees the boys and knows what he's gonna do
They fink der bad with their gang
He's got a switch of personality like ying yang
Walks up, looks sharp
Hood up, hands in pocket
He's got a knife, he's always wanted to rock it
Pulls it out, the boys shout
Then he blacks out
Snaps out, looks up
One down here, one down there
Blood everywhere
Runs home, his mum's watching Big Brother
Hides under the cover and cries
Thinking sooner or later it will be him
That will be saying his last goodbyes.
Think!
Speak out!

Connor Thorpe (14)

Someone Like You

I walk down the road, gazing at the sunlight
Wond'ring about, what love truly looks like
As you walk by, catching my eye.

My heart rate jumps, to a million miles a fortnight
Wishing that I could be the one that you liked
Life would be easy, with you by my side.

Life would be a song

I'm reaching out for rhythm
Looking out for lyrics
Searching for someone like you.

You turn your head, and throw at me that sweet smile
I smile right back, wanting you to be mine
But I'm nothing special, so you walk on by.

I reawaken, as you turn away and leave me
Realising that, you have the power over me
You sung love's tune, now I'm under your spell.

But life is just a song

Reaching out for rhythm
Looking out for lyrics
Searching for someone like you
I'm singing till my heart breaks
To make the point I wanna make
That I need someone like you!

Anna Spearing-Ewyn (16)

Life Story

Introduction
Listen to this tale very closely,
About the things I lost,
And the things that are close to me.

Verse
I remember the day 'cause it was so damn cold,
I was sitting in a corner only 14 years old
When a boy came to me and told me his name,
And I knew from that moment it would never be the same.

I took his hand and looked into his eyes,
And what I loved most is they were as blue as the sky
He held me close to the warmth of his heart,
And we beat in sync; I knew we'd never be apart.

He told me he would take me away from this place,
That I would never have to see another angry face.
He told me that everything would be alright,
And that I would never have to be afraid of the night.

Chorus
I will never forget how he turned my life around,
How he taught me to put my feet flat on the ground
I now have no pain or fear inside,
And I will never ever have to run away or hide,
I now know how to be happy and free,
And what keeps me going is his love for me.

Ffion Davies (14)

Life And The Teen

So how long shall I wait,
For you to come around?
Cos I'm losing my grip,
To stand on stable ground.
Nothing's worse but things do take their toll
And still decide to fall.

So how do you plead,
Guilty on your knees?
With your hands held up high,
Reaching towards the sky.
No one's perfect and you're no exception,
So go and take your bow.

So how far will you go,
Until you hit the unknown?
Ten more miles down this road,
Leading where God only knows.
Here's your chance, take it while you can
Before it's all too late.

So will you be the one,
To sweep me off my feet?
With your charm, arm in arm,
With words that flow so sweet?
Here I am, take my hand and fly me away.

Here I am, take my hand and fly me away.

Natasha Smith (17)

Mum, What Ya Yelling At?

Hey Mum, what ya yelling at?
So what's it for, what ya yelling at?
Hey Mum, what ya yelling at?
So what's it for, what ya yelling at?

OK I'll hurry up, I need to get ma trousers on
Need to get ma shirt on
Need to get ma tie on
And need to get ma blazer on
Then I'll go and brush ma teeth
Then I'll go and brush ma hair
Then I'll put it in a bobble
Then I'll come downstairs.

Hey Mum, what ya yelling at?
So what's it for, what ya yelling at?
Hey Mum, what ya yelling at?
So what's it for, what ya yelling at?

Came home from school and then ma mum said,
'What you do today?'
'Spanish, English, science, maths and then some geography
I got a C, D, E, F and in geography I got a U.'

Hey Mum, what ya yelling at?
So what's it for, what ya yelling at?
Hey Mum, what ya yelling at?
So what's it for, what ya yelling at?

Eve Rowles (11)

Fallen Idols

Cruising the streets in custom made cars
Like prophets from God you'll see the stars
And all those desperate to be the same
With plastic bodies and a bleached blonde mane.

Stand on the corner of Hollywood Boulevard
No one's watching you enter the strip club or bar
Go on right in, you'll be sure to see them
Middle-class respectable young gentlemen

It's oh so perfect
World famous
The rich can't do wrong, who can blame us?
But there's a dark underworld
Little drug-addled girls
Blindly following a leader
Promising a positive new way of life
With violence, guns and knives.

Back in those happy, hippie days
A psychedelic dream chased reality away
Shouting green for go, seeing red
Scarlet, crimson, they're lying there dead.

That was what happened on that warm August night
A stunning young actress and her friends killed outright
Sending mixed morals and messages from the hippie era,
Peace, love and a bloody murder.

Emma Myers (16)

The Man On The Corner

Driving past, watching the world go by so fast
Everything is flying by, hardly making contact with my eyes

But I saw you, on the corner
Bottle of Corona in hand
You were looking down at the floor
At the biggest ashtray known to man

How did this happen to you?
The cute little baby toddling up and down
Oh no, what happened to you?
I remember when you told me your whole life's plans

You were gonna be a doctor, in the city of New York
You were gonna go to uni, to Cambridge I thought

But I guess that's not going to happen
You don't even have a home anymore
Begging for what you're taking
Oh, what are you doing that for?

The beard is getting longer, every time that I go past
You think the drugs are making you stronger,
But it's never going to last

And it's sad just seeing you sat there
You don't even have a home anymore
Sleeping rough on the pavement
Oh, what are you doing that for?

Clare Hurst (15)

You There . . .

We sat there,
Sat there talking,
Wondering what's going on.

You used me,
Used me for the last time.
I swear this is the end.

The only love you have,
Is for that man in the mirror.
There's no room for me.

What you did
I cannot say.
You hurt me,
Hurt me too much.

You used me.
Used me for the last time.
I swear this is the end.

I cannot go on,
Not like this.
I've left you for good.

This is the end.
You sit there,
Staring into darkness,
This is the end.

Charlotte Foster (15)

The Olympics 2012

The stadium's all ready,
The Olympians are here,
London is beaming,
This is our year.

The opening ceremony will be a grand affair,
Enjoyed by everyone including London's Lord Mayor.

The sprinters are ready,
On their marks,
Their adrenalin is flowing,
Anxious to start.

High jumps spring,
Pole vaulters fly,
The javelin gleams,
Against the blue sky.

Swimmers and sailors will all have their turn,
When they receive the gold medal,
They will stand strong and firm.

The flags are all flying in triumphant glory,
The winners will go home telling their own story.

The rain may fall,
But rainbows will rise,
The sun will break through,
Where our great city lies.

Ben Glossop (11)

Tightrope Walking

Chorus
Tightrope walking on the edge of your very last try
A clown like you cannot laugh every day of his life
Did you think that you could take something out of your hat
Create a miracle to fix your life just like that

Verse 1
What acrobatic stunt do you have now
To somehow make your whole life turn around?
How long, how long till you leave from here
A puff of smoke, a spark of fire, you disappear?

Pre chorus
You have been acting out all your life
But the performance has gone wrong
You don't know who's leading your circus
But it's a shame the show must go on

Repeat chorus

Verse 2
In a pack of cards you can't always pull out an ace
Get your make-up off and wipe that smile off your face
It went so well but then it went so wrong
It's true, the circus is not where you belong.

Repeat pre chorus:

Repeat chorus.

Jack Shephard (10)

This Is True

The day you left I watched
And hoped that one day you'd return
We sat for hours, my crying
And tired, not wanting to sleep

Me hanging out the bathroom window
You walking away to the car
You turned only once to wave to me
The last time I would see you off

My face hot from crying, eyes too heavy
I ran back to my room
Pictured you for a while
Before I drifted off into a deep sleep

That night went fast
I woke up
Face still burning red
Eyes still heavy

Hoping what went on that night
Was nothing more than a dream
I checked to see if he was there . . .

But no, my dad had gone
It truly was the last night
I saw him go

And I still miss him.

Kaylee Branch (15)

Rain Girls

I don't know how it came to be
That we would be such great friends three
We have our troubles, yes we fight,
But hopefully it's put right tonight.
As the sky fills and the rain pours in,
My ditzy friend with the name of Sim
Decided to go mad and dance in the rain,
Caroline and I, we did the same.

Honestly, I know it's crazy
But we'll be friends forever, forever maybe,
Let's dance – go nuts! – While we're young and free,
Sitting in puddles and laughing, us three.

When you're 13 and 14 everything's a drama,
Life's hard and scary 'cause we watch Panorama.
Sometimes all it takes is a laugh and a smile,
Perhaps dancing in the rain for a little while.
And as the raindrops fall from high,
I watch the world just passing by.
In this world of misery,
Could I be happy? Could I be free?

This one wet day left in my mind,
Imprinted memory standing time,
Never mind the life ahead,
I was happy when I went to bed.

Jessica Cripps (13)

Untitled

I wanted to see you
I wanted to hold you
But life goes past so fast
The times that I need you
The life that you gave me
I hope it forever lasts

Feeling free beside you
Feeling a need to be with you
Is forever my sweet thought
That touch of hope
The hope of love
Hoping life isn't too short

When the special times come
When things get rough
Then you are right there beside
Hoping for the finest
Hoping for what's desired
Wishing in my arms you died

Waiting months and years
Waiting just for you
Is like hell amongst the fire
Thinking of the good times
Thinking of our sweet life
Is what you and me desire.

Aisha Amhar (13)

I'm In Love With Her

I was driving down the street
In my Ferrari
I felt the heat
When I saw a sexy lady
She looked at me
And I began to stare

I pulled over once
I pulled over twice
She carried on walking
So I went as fast as mice
Ow baby, ooo baby, yerr baby
I'm in love with her

I got out of my car
I went up to her
By the time I was there
She was far, far
Ow baby, ooo baby
I'm in love with her

I wish I'd said something
But I didn't know what to say
She's gone now
So I guess I'll have to pay
Ow baby, ooo baby
I'm in love with her.

Jacob Rogers (13) & Beth Honour (14)

Dawn Of Peace

It's 4 o'clock, it's time to move
'Cause yeah, we've got nothing to lose
We'll run down a hill, kick a troll
Bang our head on every wall
If we do that again it's going in the bin
It ain't no sin to glance and grin
But make sure you don't pull the pin.

Brum, brum, brum, goes the tank
Thud, thud, thud, of the gun
Run, run, run, reinforcements coming your way
Boom, boom, boom, of the airborne bombs.

Away run the others, we win today
Raise that flag above the bay
Hold the line while they whine
They have lost this time but tomorrow's another day
Let's just hope we win again
We'll all feel better when we get to peace, when war is done
Why can't we live in friendship
Lay down our weapons and live together in harmony?

Brum, brum, brum, goes the tank
Thud, thud, thud, of the gun
Run, run, run, reinforcements coming your way
Boom, boom, boom, of the airborne bombs at . . .
You!

Adam Lee (12)

What's Goin' On?

I wake up one day and walk down the street,
Here's the things I do and the people I meet.

I saw my mate and he's snorted some coke,
He's gonna get addicted and I know that he's broke.
He looked up at me and offered me some,
And I said I won't touch the stuff,
He thinks I ain't tough enough.
But I ain't no fool, I ain't gonna get kicked outta my school.
Then I thought,
Hey, what's going on? Everything seems to be going wrong!

So I walked back home feeling damned depressed,
And I decided that I needed a rest.
So I turned on the TV and changed to the news,
And upstairs I can hear my brother playing blues.
So the reporter is in Afghanistan,
She's talkin' about a guy who's called Sadam.
He's blown up a cinema with a car bomb,
She says there won't be more, but it won't be long.
Then I thought,
Hey, what's going on? Everything seems to be going wrong!

And later on when I go to bed,
I can't get this stuff right out of my head.
So I begin to think what tomorrow will bring,
And I start to wonder if you'll change anything?

Simon Lange-Smith (12)

Issue 56

They're growing up too fast you see,
Well you know what they're like
So we beckon and confuse them say,
'Be healthy, ride a bike!
Lose those pounds, yet love your body!
See these models - they don't care!
Then we'll talk BMI
To make your body judgement fair!'

They're turning us and twisting us
They're leaving none untouched
So come on, enjoy the freak show
Only two pounds a month!

We have your problems on page twelve
Yes, we know all about you,
We don't encourage anything, but
Make sure everyone else do!
And then on page eleven
It's about the perfect party pout
And our prizes - they're so daily
They'll make you scream and shout!

They're turning us and twisting us
They're leaving none untouched
So come on, enjoy the freak show
Only two pounds a month!

Amelia Oliver (14)

What We've Done

The tumbling hills roamed free, before we came along.
The strong Earth turned to sea, before we made it wrong
And every sight was one so fine
And every height defied the line
There was no fight for yours or mine
Before this present age.

And then the human race started spreading through the land,
Starting to replace the wholesome beauty all around.
Land was bought and wars were fought.
Peace was thought a last resort.
Too soon we wrought the Earth distraught
Within this present age.

Now tarmac roads lie where sparkling rivers used to flow
And grass did live and die where violent buildings will now grow.
Nature's not grown but created.
Flowers are not sown but painted.
Beauty's not alone but tainted,
In this present age.

Soon the world will be no more; the Earth will turn to grey
And as we search to find the cure, we too will pass away.
And all as ghosts, we'll consider
What we were supposed to deliver,
But at its best hope is a sliver
To protect our Earth's sweet age.

Oliver Jones (15)

Life

Wasted times that you'd like to change,
Will be there forever in your mind.
Life just goes on all that way,
Until it comes to that dreadful day.

I'll do what I want whenever I want to,
I'll do it when I want, however I want to.
There's no stopping me whatever you do,
If you try to stop me, you'll really regret it.

Nobody cares what they do,
Cos you only get one chance at being you.
We got control over our own lives,
And we don't care what ya say-ay-ay.

I'll do what I want whenever I want to,
I'll do it when I want, however I want to.
There's no stopping me whatever you do,
If you try to stop me, you'll really regret it.

We may tell some petty lies,
But we take a step back into line.
We don't need none of your advice,
Cos we know when we make our mistakes.

It's my life and I got control,
I'll do what I want,
Cos it's my life!

Austin Young (12)

Mr Wrong

I thought you were with me,
But you disappeared without a trace.
I thought you were reliable,
You weren't there on the second date.
The third and fourth?
They just weren't there.
Thought it was you and me
But this is not fair!
I told my best friend what thoughts were in my head,
Turns out when you weren't with me,
You were with her instead.
We are *so* not friends no more,
My best friend is my blog.
Go on, how many more of my best friends you gonna snog?
Yeah, go on, you better hide!
I can't believe I fell
For that really obvious textbook love spell.
But now you've got nothing,
Those girls got bored and left,
Later you got arrested,
For another heart theft.
Meanwhile I found Mr Right,
And we're in love so strong,
We sit and talk and laugh at you,
We call you Mr Wrong ...

Hannah Prentice (12)

Your Life

Life isn't easy
If you're alone in the world
But you can make a difference
'Cause you are not alone
'Cause you are special
'Cause you're always yourself
If you try your best you will succeed in life
Just be yourself and have a laugh
You have your friends
They will help you come through life
If you wonder where they are
They're somewhere in the world
They will always be there for you in life
'Cause you're special
'Cause you're always yourself
If you try your best you will succeed
Just be yourself and have a laugh in life
'Cause you're special
'Cause you're always yourself
If you try your best you will succeed
Just be yourself and have a laugh in life
Making an exit in the world
Having to leave your boyfriend on Earth
To make a journey into space
To start a new life in the galaxy.

Rebecca Sokoroniec (18)

Patience For You

It would be nice if the past could return
The way I'd like it to be
My heart wouldn't have been a sufferer
And I would have been free
Ever since you went, the days just keep getting longer
However, my love for you just keeps getting stronger
I love you, love that I do dare anyone to speak of its feeling
The silent love that can't be described by any ordinary person
The love that causes a tear to fall from between the lines of these verses
Your crystal heart has warmed my heart to love you more than the roses
I want to describe my angel
How, I do not know
For all the words are just too simple and narrow
I am alone in the west whilst my soul is in the east
I must be patient and wait
For I know that soon we'll meet
Because without you I feel as though my life is being stolen
My painful tears are hard to stop and they're affecting my reason
My heart is calling by your name it's felt all kinds of emotion
So please come back
For I have an illness
I can only be cured if I see you
If I gather the whole world together
They all won't be able to tell you
How much I miss you.

Amal Ahmed (15)

You And I

Even if I try, I can't identify
which guy I really like, such a confusing life

It's been such a mess, with this whole stress
I think I need a vacation, to get my head around this situation

I love you, just thought you might want to hear it.
I'm just so into you, I just can't resist you!
It's like flying in the sky, being with you
It's like falling down apart, when I'm losing you!

I might just break down, after losing you so fast
with all of your emotions, such a confusing guy

It's been such a mess, with this whole stress
I think I need a break, to get my lines straight

I love you, just thought you might want to hear it,
I'm so into you, I just can't resist you!
It's like flying in the sky, being with you
It's like falling down apart, when I'm losing you!

But did you ever think about what might happen to both of us
when this story might end, when all this will come to an end ...

I love you, just thought you might want to hear it.
I'm just so into you, I just can't resist you!
It's like flying in the sky, being with you
It's like falling down apart, when I'm losing you!

Agata Lesniewska (13)

Destiny And Fate

I belong with you,
Whether it's right or wrong,
Destiny will choose its course,
It won't be that long,
Till they decide,
If it's meant to be,
For you and me,
To be side by side.

I'm a big believer in destiny and fate,
Not everything is handed on your plate,
You gotta fight for what's right,
Then everything will be in sight, yeah,
There's nothing too big, or nothing too small,
You will still stand very tall,
'Cause everything's gonna be alright,
And you and I hopefully might.

So please wait, give us a chance,
We can make it, I am sure,
Who else makes you feel this way?
Our love is so pure,
We will stand together, forever,
For the rest of time,
We will have the best adventure,
And discover the great climb.

Jade Llewellyn (13)

Sticks And Stones

Sometimes I want to find a corner
And just disappear
You don't know how much words harm me
Although everybody says
Sticks and stones may break my bones
Yet words will never hurt me
Your words tear through me
You've left me scarred for life

Sticks and stones may break my bones
Yet words will tear me apart
I can only be who I am
Like me or not this is who I am
I can't do what you can do
I'm not as rich as you
Not as mean either
You pride yourself with others' hate
There's not one way I can relate

The pain you've caused is never-ending
When you walk down the corridor
No one smiles
But when you walk past
I raise my head high
And let you think I couldn't care what you do
Today I'm gonna stand up to you.

Heather Lee (12)

Waiting For You

When I think of you
I look up at the stars
And wonder if you see them too
I wonder where you are

I see my teardrops falling
And I dream of you
I wish that I was with you now
Standing with you
I'm waiting for you

As I stand alone
I hear a church bell ring
Christmas morning chimes
But there's no joy without the joy you'd bring

I wonder what you're doing
If you ever think of me
If you lie and dream at night
Of things that used to be

And I see my teardrops falling
And I'm dreaming about you
And I'm wishing I was with you now
Just standing here with you
I'm waiting for you
Always waiting for you.

Kirsty Mort (13)

Just A Little Girl

Chorus
Am just a little girl
With a big imagination,
With a little world of my own,
Where I keep my feelings locked away,
From the world I am in today.

The world of crime and politicians,
With new laws and safety regulations
And a news channel which goes on all day.

Chorus
The world of gadgets and laziness,
And info at your fingertips
And food to take away.

Chorus
The world of gangs
With knives hanging around,
Making mayhem on the streets.

Am just a little girl
With a big imagination,
With a little world of my own,
Where I keep my feelings locked away,
From the world I am in today,
Because the world today is a scary place to be.

Emily Wood (12)

Unforgettable

Verse 1
I know it's over and now we're apart
I know we left it and made it worse
It was a bad beginning, a very bad start
Maybe I should have tried harder to make you stay
You were right, I was wrong
Is that what you want me to say?
It could have ended better
We could have been stronger
Been happy with bliss
You didn't have to end it like this
There are so many things you didn't have to prove
So many things you really didn't have to do.

Chorus
You didn't have to walk away
You didn't have to say goodbye
You didn't have to disagree with what I say
You didn't have to leave tonight
There's still some things that haven't finished yet
I still wish we were together
But baby, you just can't forgive and forget
You and me could have been incredible
All together unbelievable
And now our memories are unforgettable. (Unforgettable x 2)

Lizzy Begg (14)

All Cried Out

There comes a time in your life when you look back at all the hurt
And I saw you the other day and remembered you treated me like dirt
How could you do that to me, I loved you with all my heart
I thought you felt the same about me
I was upset for a while, like it was the end of the world
My mind grew and began to realise I was better off without you
And then I pulled myself together
I could do way better than you
I was strong and you were wrong
And I hate you with all my heart

You expect me to cry, but I'll tell you one thing now
I am over you, you mean nothing to me just like I meant to you.

I'll carry on with my life like you never existed
You are my past, I am my present and my new binding future.
Do you still expect me to cry?
But I'm telling you I won't ...

Because I'm all cried out
No more tears left to fall
You abused me and you used me
And you tore my heart apart
You said sorry, like you thought all this hurt would go away
But you abused me and you used me
And you'll not do that anymore.

Rebbecca Widdowson (16)

Don't Leave Me Tonight

I know that times have been hard
for the both of us lately
And everything I say
Seems to make this worse
But when you slam the door
And leave your hate behind you
I realise just how much you mean to me ...

Your voice is like an angel to my ears
Your eyes can melt my heart out baby
Oh, c'mon don't you realise
that we're not meant to be apart
So honey ... don't leave me tonight.

You've told me before not to let the cat out darling,
And I know I should have ironed that shirt
But none of that really matters
anymore now baby
Cos you've stolen my heart...

Your voice is like an angel to my ears
Your eyes can melt my heart out, baby, yeah
Oh so c'mon baby don't you realise
that we're not meant to be apart
So honey ... don't leave me tonight
So honey ... don't leave me tonight.

Eleanor Hodgson (11)

212

Starlight And Laughter

There is no real love meant for you, just another at your feet,
At your call or at your favour. You never could be true
For you are starlight, you are laughter.

And I've tried and I've tried and I've tried to tell you
You never get anywhere by getting everything
And I've cried and I've sighed and I've laid down and died
But you listen to the music; you stand right up and sing.

There is no life left in you now, there is no soul left in to give,
Just some ashes and some embers. You can't take your final bow
For you are starlight, you are laughter.

And I've tried and I've tried and I've tried to tell you
You never get anywhere by getting everything
And I've cried and I've sighed and I've laid down and died
But you listen to the music; you stand right up and sing.

You get hooked on the starlight, live for the limelight
And laugh at your army of fools
You get by on the sunshine, get high on the moonshine
Love nothing but cliques all bejewelled.

You're starlight and laughter, starlight and laughter,
With your head in the silver-lined clouds.
You're starlight and laughter, starlight and laughter,
And you died on the stage for the crowd.

Jennifer Bloomfield (17)

I'll Never Forget You

Why, every time that I think of you,
I shed the same tear,
As the years have passed,
But I feel that you're still here.

And I wait for you,
And I call for you,
And I still need you,
But you're not here.

Oh, I'll always miss you,
And your memories are mine.

One day we'll be together,
We'll catch up with the memories we missed
And I won't let you go again,
We'll be happy just like I wished.

And I wait for you,
And I call for you,
And I still need you,
But you're not here.

Yeah, I still need you,
But you're not here,
Oh I'll always miss you,
And your memories are mine.

Lauren Horner (13)

Puppet

Lost within, I cannot breathe
Change; release your hold on me.
And there's so many people dying, and we're losing our time for crying
Change or let go, the choice cannot be mine.

I am myself, I am the only one.
I am myself I cannot change for you.
You put me down and you say that I must stay.
But I am myself and I cannot forgive you.

Mind slows down but time won't cease.
Hate seems strong inside of me.
Why are there people crying, and why is there no one trying?
You have to let go, but the choice cannot be mine.

I am myself, I am the only one.
I am myself I cannot change for you.
You put me down you say that I must stay.
But I am myself and I cannot forgive you.

I am myself and I'll be that only one.
I am myself I will not change for you.
You dress me up and you say that I must play
But I am myself and I cannot begin for you.

I'm sick of you all deciding; my life is my own for writing
I know I have to let go, but this choice must be mine ...

Shashia Mitchell (17)

A Final Opportunity

Into - Guitars + Clarinet
A final opportunity
A dream come true
It's all I ever wanted . . . from you

A lasting memory
A chance to say goodbye
If only . . . there was time

Chorus
My idol, my only one
You slipped away
Destiny is calling you
It wouldn't, it couldn't . . . let you stay

Instrumental
Another inspiration
Here we are again
When will there be another . . . like you?

A heart that is broken
There's no escape
You have left us . . . to go our way

Chorus
Repeats and slows down.

**Fiona Sutherland (15), Georgia Matchett, Elizabeth Dawes
& Katie Wassel**

Move It Like You Feel It

The music's playing loud and lively,
Been here all night but not leaving early,
There's more to it than I thought before,
But all I wanna do is have fun on the dance floor,
Just move it and forget the rest,
I know I'm not all you think about,
So why don't you prove it?
Why don't you move it like you feel it with me?
The night's progressing onto more than I wanted,
You're telling me things I don't need to hear,
When all I want to do is shake the night away,
Stay up dancing till late with who seems to be more than a mate.
Just move it and forget the rest,
I know I'm not all you think about,
So why don't you prove it?
Why don't you move it like you feel it with me?
Yeah, you mean so much to me,
It's true I care, I really do,
You say you're falling in love,
Just push it to the side and let this night take you to paradise.
Why don't you relax and feel the beat?
You should realise I'm not what you need,
Perhaps you should leave things be,
Why don't you move it like you feel it with me?

Charlotte Broughton (13)

Life's Test

Listen in for the lies of a truthful tale,
Look for the time that changed your life,
Now's the time to make a stand against your enemy,
    All this hate inside of me,
    All this love that's wasting me
    I need to prove I'm strong enough to hold myself above the rest,
    To prove myself in this life's test.
All my life I've been known as the nobody,
But now it's changed and I don't know what to do.
I'm not used to all this attention,
I have the friends and family I need for what I am to do.
    All this hate inside of me,
    All this love that's wasting me
    I need to prove I'm strong enough to hold myself above the rest,
    To prove myself in this life's test.
One year later, I look inside of me, thinking who I am,
I've got the attention, I want more, I can't find it,
I found the lies in a truthful tale,
The time that changed your life is now . . .
I made the stand, I lost the fight and now's the time to start again.
    All this hate inside of me,
    All this love that's wasting me
    I need to prove I'm strong enough to hold myself above the rest,
    To prove myself in this life's test.

Curtis Cronin (14)

Hey Stranger

Not seen you in so long
Hope you're still going strong
Been missing round here
Put on your cowboy gear
My little Texas ranger
Love makes us, shakes us, breaks us
And you don't even realise.
Love takes us, fakes us, wakes
Why can't you open your eyes?
They say the wicked die young
So you've got time, my son
You life will wait for you
C'mon, relax now stranger.
I guess this was fun
But now our time is done
I know your hands are tied
See you on the other side
When you get out of danger
Love for you my stranger
Cos love made us, shook us, broke us
I should have realised.
Love took us, faked us, woke us,
I shouldn't have opened my eyes.
Not so strange now, stranger.

Anna Spence (13)

That Boy

He's the sweet smell she loves,
the one who calls you beautiful
when she's looking rough.
He's the tears streaming out of those bright blue eyes,
the reason for upset and sleepless nights.
But he's the good, the bad, the ugly, perfect
perfect, he's part of her, her life, so what should she do?
'You can do better, he's an idiot,' her friends say
but are they the ones who light her up like a summer's day?
He breaks her trust,
but is forgetting him a must?
He's the one that makes her angry,
He says, 'I love you,' and she wants to part with him no longer.
He's the smile cheek to cheek on her face,
the one who's already won first place.
He's the one, who makes sure she's alright,
the one who cuddles her till the end of daylight
He makes her smile, makes her happy
makes her cry, makes her angry
makes her feel like hitting the gin,
then he gives her that loved up, childhood grin
and she realises
he's the good, the bad, the ugly, the beautiful.
He's part of her, her life.

Cassie-Louise Holdsworth (16)

Friends Forever

'Cause you went and changed my mind forever
Never told me now or never
We will be together
'Cause, we are friends forever
No matter what the weather
I don't care as long as my friends are there
By my side
Things come in and things go out
Your life gets turned upside down
But as long as you've got friends
They'll help you make it till the end
People come and people go
It just shows you what they know
They help you through the ups
And they help you through the downs
We are friends forever 'cause
They help you through the smiles
And they help you through the frowns
Every day's a new story
Every day's a new glory
No matter what you do
Your friends will be there too
Because they are friends forever
And they'll help me through whatever.

Abigail Norton (13)

Just One Kiss

I know everything about you, that's how much I love you
My heart pounds for you like no other
They all say I'm a mad woman
Cos I fall in love every time I see you
You want to come, but you can't right now
You just make me hypnotised
Just one kiss a day

Let's go away, away from this town
You're so lovely
Or have you got another?
Got to know if we can go
I just need to know
Cos I love you so much
You're so amazing
The smallest of things can change our own lives

Don't tell me you love another
Cos you know I'm the one you dream of
There is no doubt we're made for each other
They think I'm all for your money
I know there is someone stopping you coming
You want to come, but you can't right now
You just make me hypnotised
Just one kiss a day.

Sasha Yates (12)

A Slave To Their Ways

In my life,
Mistakes have been made,
The friends I've chosen,
And the friends I've began to hate,
Their behaviour to others,
And the way they treat their mates,
I don't want to become
A slave to their ways.

Don't get brainwashed,
In being one of the crowd,
Be humble,
Not stupid and loud,
'Cause everyone has a mind,
A mind to speak what's wrong and what's right,
I don't want to become
A slave to their ways.

Don't sob and don't you cry,
'Cause I will live my life the way I like,
I have my friends and you have yours,
I am done and finished,
Had enough of your ways,
'Cause I don't want to become
A slave to your ways.

Georgia Mae Heard (13)

You Are . . .

You are my sunshine,
You are my sky,
You are the love and the hate
And the teardrops that I cry.
And if God is everywhere, then
You are inside,
Because you are the one
In whom I always can confide.

You are my daisies,
You are my field,
You are the joy and the faith
You're my own beautiful shield.
Because you are a rainbow
But I am a cloud
And you are the one
Who will stand out from the crowd.

You are my ice cream,
You are my pear,
You are the life and the soul
And the good times we could share.
And if you are a dark night
Then you're also a star,
Because you still look shining from afar.

Hannah Taylor (12)

Missing You

Chorus
There's something inside me
I don't understand
It's making me dizzy
It's driving me mad
I only get this feeling
When I've been with you
This feeling inside me
Is missing you

Verse 1
You make me feel so small
And I sometimes wonder why I ever loved you at all
I don't want to see you
Cos all you do is make me cry
Your face, your smile, your everything
Makes me wonder why

Verse 2
You really didn't care
When you broke my heart and left me standing there alone
I hope that you're happy
I hope she's everything I'm not
I'll be the girl that you forgot
No need to say goodbye.

Alice Singleton (16)

Make The Best Of Your Life

Every day I wonder what life will be, where will it take me?
Seeing all these people doing crimes on TV
And I know this city is not the future for me
But I just say, I just say

Chorus
Make the best, make the best of your life
Do what you want, do what you can
But always make the best, make the best
Make the best of your life while you can

If you want a decent job in life,
Go to school, do your work
And God, I pray to you,
Give me the best of life
And I know one day my life will be extraordinary

So God give me that day
God give me that day today
Every day I say, every day I say

Chorus
Make the best, make the best of your life
Do what you want, do what you can
But always make the best, make the best
Make the best of your life while you can.

Theodore Christou (13)

Without You

How can I live without you?
The one who makes me red,
How can I cope without you?
I feel as if I'm dead.

How can I be without you?
I just can't let you go,
How can I cope without you?
I'm feeling so damn low.

But I will carry on,
Along life's well-walked track
And I will carry on
Until I have you back!

How can I smile without you?
You who gives me joy,
How can I care without you?
I'm the world's loneliest boy!

But I will carry on,
Along life's well-walked track
And I will carry on
Until I have you back.
I will carry on
Until I have you . . . back.

Tom Owens (14)

Maybe It's You

Sometimes I feel so lonely,
It makes me sad inside to think
About all the things we were planning and how they're now in a ditch.

It's so sad, how did you make me so mad? ... oh oh
Please tell me

What did I ever do? I feel so confused.
What did I ever say, to make you feel this way?
Have you ever thought, just one little thought ... ?
Maybe it's you ...

... I always seem to take the blame,
It's always me that bears the pain.
Through fights we find it's me, not you, and I'm always left to explain.

I'm so mad,
How has this turned out so bad?
... Please tell me ...

Can you not accept that concept?
Ohh baby, it's over between you and me,
There's just one last thing to say.

All these times I was right you were wrong,
You were listening to a different song,
And now you better not get in my way 'cause ... I'm moving out today.

Georgia Lottie Misselbrook (13)

Just Because I Love You

I would go to the ends of the Earth just to see your smile
I would hold your hand if only for a little while
I would capture the sun, the moon and the stars just for you
I would do all of this just because I love you.
But you see, my head and my heart are telling me
not to fall in love, but I can't help the way I feel about you
Just because I love you
Just because I love you
We would hold hands and make footprints in the sand
We would watch the tide roll in and the waves come crashing down
We would watch the sunset rise and set again
We would do all of this just because we're in love
But you see, my head and my heart are telling me
not to fall in love but I can't help the way I feel about you
Just because I love you
Just because I love you
I would rearrange the stars just to spell your name
but I don't know if you feel the same
But I've got you and you've got me
can't you see that we are supposed to be?
But you see my head and my heart are telling me
not to fall in love but I can't help the way I feel about you.

I love you!

Annie-May Adams (15)

Killing Me

What's your problem?
I'm not some circus freak.
Just leave me alone,
'Cause my heart is gonna break.
Why, why, why
Is life so hard
And yet death is easy?

Can't you see, you're killing me
With your heartless personality,
Sticks and stones may break my bones
But your words never fail to hurt me.

Trapped in a memory,
I wish you were still here.
What have you done?
Are you really worth my tears?
Why, why, why
Do I miss you
When all you did was hurt me?

Can't you see, you're killing me
With your heartless personality,
Sticks and stones may break my bones
But your words never fail to hurt me.

Beth Goldthorpe (13)

Too Hard

It's just too hard, no matter what I think,
I just keep goin' no matter what it takes -
Ooh, ooh, aah,
Would you ever think, how hard it is . . .
No, you don't, no you don't,
Cos I did it all by myself . . .
It's just too harddddd . . .
Ooh, ooh, aah.

Jakaria Mohammed (11)

Untitled

The cars are shooting stars racing through the night,
The rain bends before us, in flight,
The planets bend above us, the roots beneath our feet,
The words bend around us, 'cause this is how we meet.

Walking through the artists' minds
And following the maps of men,
Tracing the fingertips of buildings
We live in. Words
Refracted in mirrors of infinity,
Stretched by the laws of gravity,
Are molecules
Binding me to you
And you to me.

The planets bend above us, the roots beneath our feet,
The words bend around us, 'cause this is how we meet.

And we can't understand
All the accents on this page,
Like we're a billion actors
Playing on a stage,
But it's words, they're words,
Molecules that bind
Making up our m-i-n-d minds.

Claire Ewbank (17)

Untitled

Feel the starlight shine around you
The warmth in the air
Feel the stardust wrap around you
Shooting stars everywhere
See them shine down upon us
Lighting the night sky
See them glisten and sparkle
The stardust lies with you . . .

Hannah Pritchard (15)

Just The Way Things Are

Well, that's just the way things are, it must be told,
But I know there's still a chance even though we're getting old.
One day our dreams will all come true,
I hope you know I'll never give up on you.
The sun is setting and it's getting dark,
Telling stories of our pasts,
Got me wondering how life's got so hard,
Well, that's just the way things are.

And as we look back we start to see,
All of those things that could have been,
But after all that's been and done,
You're still the one,
You'll always be the one for me.

It breaks my heart to see you cry,
So I put on a brave face and a smile,
Tell you it's gonna be alright,
Cos that's just the way things are.

And as we look back we start to see,
All of those things that could have been,
But after all that's been and done,
You're still the one,
Always be the one for me.

Harvey Lee (17)

Hot

It's so hot tonight but that's not
what's keeping me up all night
it's the thought of the future oh, oh, oh

Chorus
I don't know what tomorrow will be like,
so I'm thinking for today
so I just got to tell you boy
I've loved you since the day we met
we are meant to be
so what do you say?
I'm trying so hard to sleep in this heat
But the thought of you is keeping me up tonight

Chorus
Coz you're the only one that I can depend on
and the thought of you and me
together we're meant to be
I can't be without you boy
forever will be, so what do you say?

Chorus
It's so hot tonight but that's not
the reason I can't sleep
ahhhhh I can't sleeeep.

Lorraine Meekings (14)

We Might As Well Just Give Up

Verse 1
Been staring all my worries directly in the eye,
I gotta face my fears; I need a shoulder to cry on,
I need someone, to help me find my way.

Chorus
We're never gonna get this right,
We'll never figure all this out,
Our time has come for us tonight,
The love with us has been and gone,
We're over; yeah we're more than done,
So we might as well just give up. (x2)

Verse 2
With every flash of lightning, it shatters all my confidence,
And every time the thunder crashes, I realise now,
I'll find you somehow, if I finally find the love.

Repeat chorus
We're never gonna get this right,
We'll never figure all this out,
Our time has come for us tonight,
The love with us has been and gone,
We're over; yeah we're more than done,
So we might as well just give up. (x2)

Chloe Subitte (13)

Sorry

It's the hardest word to say
But my courage must prevail,
So I'm sorry for my leaving
When you were weak and frail,
No, you hadn't broke a bone
Or fractured your spine,
It was me who did the damage,
But it will heal in all due time.

Oh, I shouldn't have broken your heart,
But doesn't a lie hurt much more than the truth?
I think it was the right thing to do.

Yeah, it's the hardest word to say
Like trying to fight the rain,
But I must apologise
For leaving you in pain,
No, you hadn't broke a bone
Or fractured your spine,
It was me who did the damage
But it will heal in all due time.

Oh, I shouldn't have broken your heart,
But doesn't a lie hurt much more than the truth?
I think it was the right thing to do.

Georgia Fay (13)

Totally!

You're totally out of the question,
You're totally out of this world,
Who knows what to do with you?
You're totally wild!

But I see myself falling,
See myself breaking,
As I realise I'm falling in love.

You're totally out of control,
You're totally out of my league,
No one knows what you're up to,
You're totally wild!

But I see myself falling,
See myself breaking,
As I realise I'm falling in love.

You're totally out of their reach,
You're totally out of their sight,
I have now realised one thing,
You are now totally mine.

And now that I've fallen,
Now that I'm broken,
I know I have fallen in love.

Roxy Swindell (12)

Baby I Like You

Baby I like you
Words can't explain how I feel
But I like you
I think that says enough

Do you like me too?
The way you look at me
Gives me a clue, that
You like me too

Baby I like ya
Baby I like ya
But what can I say
We can't be together, every day

My love for you
Is in my heart
And our love will never be
Ripped apart

Coz I love you
And you love me
Together we can be happy

Baby I like ya
Baby I like ya, yeah!

Delia Leoni Montgomerie (13)

The Bear

A raging bull with claws,
patrolling the forest,
scratching it's furry back,
like a hunter searching for a kill,
with its sharp white teeth,
ripping apart the helpless rabbit,
as ruthless as a Rottweiler,
chasing and tearing apart its prey,
Its razor sharp claws,
ready to rip apart anything,
as aware as a hawk looking for its prey,
strolling around the damp, overgrown forest,
It disappears into the trees,
running like a cheetah,
chasing the petrified prey,
running as if in the Grand National,
like an animal chasing the first food in weeks,
with the wind racing through its coat,
savaging the helpless prey
now gracefully walking away,
with the helpless prey in its mouth,
the razor sharp claws,
searching for another kill.

Andrew Innes (13)

Unique

I'm just me,
I can't change,
Call me what you wish,
It hurts and I'm breaking inside,
I breathe in my pain from this world,
And I carry on,
But,
Why don't you kiss my wrists?
Cos your lips are like razor blades.
Sometimes I feel I need to quit,
So Dad was right,
You can't trust anyone,
Cos they will all ruin you.
Maybe I should have listened to his advice,
'Baby, you don't need to be different,
You're amazing being unique.'
So maybe I should have listened,
Cos if I did,
I wouldn't be hurting like I am.
I sit in the corner and cry,
I let my sorrow release itself,
I'm just unique,
Why can't people accept that?

Maria West (13)

Government, Stop Wasting My Time

Government, stop wasting my time
Every day someone commits another crime
From Manchester, the capital crime city
To London where there's pity and gritty
You say in your meetings to posh little friends
That from now on crime will end
But the next day when I turn on the news
I see another youth's died through being abused
By a knife or a gun or someone's bad temper
But whatever the issue things aren't getting better
Because when someone gets shot or stabbed in a rundown city
By the time the ambulance gets there
Their heart has stopped beating
And the one who committed the crime thinks they're 'even Stevens'
When they get a jail sentence and a couple of beatings
These days there's not enough tissues to wipe the mothers' tears away
The government say sorry but then it happens again
From London town to New York city crime's polluting the cities
Shanks and guns are attractions, no one's taking no action
These days the government's promises mean nothing
Now I know that they are just bluffing
And it's more than a shame because there's a heart filled with pain again.

Amber Maurice (13)

No Dreams Fade Away

Once you gave me the word,
Write down the lyrics that you heard,
In your mind, spirit, soul.
Set them free on the blank page ahead.
The human spirit wants to explore,
To see what's out in this world,
Why live in this one place so bare
When it's a whole adventure out there.
Open a trap door,
Over the lands, skies and sea,
If I will fall or soar,
Will it make any sense to me?
Now's the time to get the journey right,
Never take the dream out of sight.
Look to the stars and be free,
This is my time for them to shine down on me.
Always smiling, always shining,
I know the feeling will never fade,
Because I know I've found the way.
I've finally seen the light of day,
Never let that same dream fade away,
Never reach the endless drive,
Until I know the dream is right.

Naomi Morris (16)

Forever Is Overrated

I rant, moan, quote and write.
It's all over.
Nothing I know will stop anything.
I don't know,
Even thinking of you rings alarm bells.
I want things to change, but that's my dream
And it's selfish so I keep it to myself.
I don't want to spoil it for anyone,
I'm not going to do anything,
Because if I do it'll spoil a friendship which
Is utterly different to anything I've come across before.
So you don't see this but it is,
It's there, something different,
Or maybe you just aren't allowed to see it.
Either way, one day you will.
Until that day,
I'll write and write, until there's nothing left
And I'll quote, but never moan because it hurts everyone.
So I may rant from time to time,
But if I don't let off the anger that you've caused,
It'll hurt you as well as me.
Nothing will last forever,
Forever is overrated.

Natalie Peaston (15)

Gonna Explode!

'I'm gonna explode across the world
Gonna blow everything in my way deep into space'

DJ Pencil in the house! He's scratchin' the decks!
Ruler and pen lid boogie all night!

'I'm gonna explode across the world
Gonna blow everything in my way deep into space'

AJ Rubber's burnin' a hole on the dance floor!
Lil bro Stapler shootin' 'em out over the dance floor!
The music's loud baby, yeah,
What to do, what to sing, where to go?

DJ Protractor in the house hiding behind the mixing desk
Ooh yeah, scratch the decks, mix the music!
Hear the ducks quack, the dogs bark and the cat miaow
(Decks scratch) DJ Pencil joins in! Yeah!

DJ Pencil in the house! He's scratchin' the decks!
Ruler and pen lid boogie all night!

'I'm gonna explode across the world
Gonna blow everything in my way deep into space'

You can dance, you can jive
Having the time of your life.

Luke Portas (11)

Jealous

Take the easy road
leave my troubles behind
take this opportunity
and I'll smile with my eyes
I can get through this
I will prove I can be stronger
I won't look back on the old days
just concentrate on the future.

It won't just be about
the actions I take
It will be about
the words I speak too

I don't have to mind
what people say to me
I'll act like I don't care
make them feel like a freak
I will take the credit
I will laugh it off
be happy with who I am
won't change for them
because you know what?
They're jealous.

Andessa Martin (13)

You Were Made For Me

I stared into your eyes and deep down I knew that was the end
My aching heart didn't wanna accept it, but me and you both knew we had to
do it.
What we had was worth fighting for, but we didn't in the end,
Both sides of the battle were lost and when your heart is fully broken, it never
seems to mend.

Broken dreams, shattered hopes, all blown away in the wind,
So careless but so thinkingly selfless we let it slip away
And in the blink of an eye the magic we shared
The laughter turned to pain, tears so unprepared,
Never thought it would end this way, never thought it could end this way,
But all we ever fought for, disappeared, leaving dismay.

Reflecting on the time we spent, it was all so sudden, but nothing kept us
apart,
Like a forest fire, on a clear blue day, we stood out from the crowd, with the
kinda love we made,
People backed away from these feelings inside,
But we were never afraid to let them shine.
Time slowly ticks by and there's still no change,
But there's still hope inside me that there will come that day
When you realise this was meant to be, that I was made for you,
And you were made for me.

Laura MacPherson (14)

First Love And Loss

We met when we were only fourteen,
You played guitar while I played tambourine,
I saw you looking but I was too shy,
You didn't realise that you'd caught my eye.
And so we went on for a while,
Acting like nothing was going on,
But then I fell in love with your smile,
And your hair, and your eyes, and your ...

We fell in love when we were fifteen,
You were the cutest thing I'd ever seen,
You took me to all your favourite places,
I showed you all my favourite faces.
We'd kiss till day turned to night,
We'd talk and laugh and hardly ever fight.

You moved away when we were sixteen,
It was the saddest place I'd ever been,
I cried every day for six weeks,
I had permanent tear stains on my cheeks.
You'd call and sometimes you'd write,
But eventually you lost sight,
Of me and our relationship,
That was my first love, that was it.

Jessie Smith (14)

I Wish I Knew

More responsibility resting on my shoulders
I'm growing up, I'm getting older.
My social time is getting less and less,
As I strive to achieve success.
Got lots of decisions to make,
Hope I don't make a mistake …

Decisions – what shall I do?
Commitments – I've got quite a few.
Balance – hard to find, it's true.
Future – what to do? I wish I knew.

I've got options to pick,
I can ditch the lessons I couldn't stick.
Gotta think about what I want to be,
In 10 years time, where do I see me?
Got lots of decisions to make,
Hope I don't make a mistake …

Decisions – what shall I do?
Commitments – I've got quite a few.
Balance – hard to find, it's true.
Future – what to do? I wish I knew.

Yeah, I wish I knew.

Ellen Bishop (14)

Simply Babes (I Could Not Stay)

Oh why did you have to make things so hard? Uh huh
Why did you have to stir it all up? Uh huh
I mean we were fine at first
But now it seems that we are cursed
And everything is going for the worst. Uh huh

And you said, 'Please don't leave me, not today'
But I really, really cannot stay
What you do, it drives me mad
So now I'm going and I'm so glad.

And now it seems I'm running faster than ever
Cos I can't stand us being together
I need to get away
Cos simply babes, I could not stay.

And you said, 'Please don't leave me, not today'
But I really, really cannot stay
What you do, it drives me mad
So now I'm going and I'm so glad.

Yeah, now I've gone I feel much better
And yesterday I got your letter
So I'm sorry you're upset I left that day
But simple babes, I could not stay!

James Land (13)

Summer Days

You'd look at me, my stomach would flutter
'I love you,' you'd constantly mutter
your soul was as beautiful as a blanket of snow
whilst your walk was as graceful as a doe.

Our hearts entwined like man to breath,
like I knew it would, when we first met.

Summer days, long and gone
how my heart pleads for one
whose name caresses my soul,
my only, my all.

Your majestic voice would bow heads,
my heart was set on the day we'd wed.

Summer days, long and gone
how my heart pleads for one
whose love burned like the sun.

Now, my day half flies without you,
by my side whispering sweet nothings in my ear,
now things I long to hear.

Summer days I held so dear,
knowing you were always near.

Chinedu Agwu (15)

What's The Point?

What's the point of trying when you just keep on lying?
Why can't you just tell me the truth?
Come on baby, now listen to your heart
what is it saying to you?
I just want to know one thing,
does it hurt to know that you're losing me because of your lies?
Now do you see that not everything to me could be so bad?
Can't you see how sad it's making me?
My heart is breaking me in two.
Too many tears are falling from my eyes
and they're falling so fast I can hardly see.
I have no choice but to let them fall,
from where the pain is killing me,
Slowly, down deep, that I just can't breathe,
So can someone please save me?

Can someone please just help me?
I feel like I'm falling so fast.
I just need to stop a minute and breathe.
I need help more than you think, I just want to help you see the truth
you can tell me anything
I just want you to see what's right in front of you,
because if not, what's the point in the truth?

Toni Ashley Casteel (15)

Untitled

Hold me close, take my hand, one last dance.
Hold me close, cradle me, one last chance.
Oh my baby, please stay,
Oh my baby, don't go away.
The wind has changed your mind but
Hold me close, take my hand, one last dance
Hole me close, cradle me, one last chance.
Till my heart breaks
Take a chance!

Lucy Mackintosh (13)

Powerless

In the ever-pressing darkness of my world,
Single sparks of meaning kept attention turned,
But when I saw him walking by,
In the brightness of his eyes, the lights they dimmed and died,
I want him with a thirst that can't be quelled.

But I look on high,
And I can but sigh,
'Cause I know I can never ever have him belong with me.

Love makes me feel so powerless, powerless, powerless.

So many times I thought I saw myself deep in his mind,
But now I realise
He sees nothing.

Why must I be so powerless, powerless, powerless?

In his heart there is no place for me.
I've lost it now.

Powerless, powerless, powerless.

No lights are left to guide me back to reality.
Darkness has conquered me.

And I'm powerless.

Lily Taylor (15)

Departure From Life

Everybody has to die someday and millions of people die everyday
but their beloved ones always pray
'Please don't die,' they say this while they cry
each tear drops like a petal
but outside they're really gentle
but inside there is deep pain and misery
because they have been separated from their friends, relatives and family
before they used to live happily
now they live miserably.

Vrindavani Dasa (11)

Sugar Glass Jar

Sitting staring at the sky
Watching, as the stars go by
there's a path across the universe
it's been there since time's birth
now I run and dance along it
whilst the moon plays a folk tune,
on a wooden flute

I want to steal a star
and hide it in a sugar glass jar
where I will look at it every day
to make sure its light never fades away

While the rain falls
I hear a wild bird's call
as the rain starts to ebb
a spider weaves a gossamer web
and flowers bloom
in the light of the moon

I've stolen a star
and hidden it in a sugar glass jar
where I look at it every day
making sure that it never fades away.

Helena Jarman (15)

Poetry In Motion

This love is a tragedy,
Like a Shakespeare with no comedy.
A love story like Romeo and Juliet
But to kill yourself,
Well, I would never let it.

If I were to write
You a haiku, it would be
About me and you.

A song is like poetry in motion,
Like a lullaby with a little more notion.
It's a sonnet
When you want it.
I'm not over you,
Guess I never will be,
Feel like I'm
Stuck in poetry.

When I'm down,
I write a song over you,
And when you're
Not around,
It stops me from feeling so blue.

Hannah Simmons (16)

Smile

Tick-tock, tick-tock, I'm bored
Watching the rain I snore, I snore
But then I jump, smile, move around
Click my feet to the beat
And make a sound and smile
Grin with a cheeky grin
I smile, jump to my feet
And do it all neat
I smile, all I can do is smile
Just for a little while
When I feel the buzz in my feet
It really hits the beat
Joking all the time
'Cause smiling's not a crime
I smile, smile, smile, smile
It's a healthy lifestyle with a smile
So jump, smile, shake around
Do it to the beat as it hits the sound
So when the music is on if you're bored
Smile, jump around the place
With your grinning smile
Oh, just smile!

Hayley Bacon (11)

Can You Believe In This?

What cannot be saved is a single falling teardrop
What cannot be stopped is a cry of despair
What is coming is a chain of hatred
Friendship . . . can you believe in this?

What confuses you are the footsteps of regret
What chases you are the gazes of suspicion
What wanders through is your other self
Shattered memories . . . can you believe in this?

The sounds of footsteps are whispers from the past
What you see if just reality in the mist
What you hear is forgiveness for you
Apology . . . can you believe in this?

What has arrived is the evening twilight
What has been lost is the darkness in time
What met in the middle is the space between the past and future
Responsibility . . . can you believe in this?

What you touch is a quivering image
What's resigning are the echoes of sadness
What you smell are you smouldering memories
Promise . . . can you believe in this?

Lynsey Pioli (13)

Once I Was That Girl

Once I was that girl,
No one could understand me,
I can't believe it's true,
It's just me. (x 2)

No one ever talks to me,
I was so lonely,
I don't understand why,
No one has been this lonely.

Once I was that girl,
No one could understand me,
I can't believe it's true,
It's just me. (x 2)

Why has it got to be me?
I can't understand.
It seems like I'm different,
Now I feel like I can't stand.

Once I was that girl,
No one could understand me,
I can't believe it's true,
It's just me. (x 2)

Holly Jewell (12)

Flying Solo

I remember
So many years ago
When a single word echoed,
Echoed, echoed across the dawn

One dark December
So many tears ago
The word 'love' brought my world crashing down,
Come crashing, crashing to the ground

But when I think of all the words that you ever said to me
And when I think of all the promises I ever said to you
How many are dead and gone?
And how many still live on?
Do I deserve it all?
That's love

Nobody said it was easy
Well, nobody lied
And nobody cried

Nobody asked you the reason
They just left you to fly
Alone you will die.

Sean Guggiari (16)

Angel

Laid here wondering where you are
Under the stars at night,
Just thinking about you all the time
Can't get you out my mind.

The moonbeams shine down on me,
Strange moonlight on the ground.
I wonder if you thought of me
When you left, making no sound.

You never gave a reason
Why you left me lying here,
Under the stars which we looked up at
And saw a thousand years.

It's almost as if you weren't real,
Just a smile and sweet words.
The tears are falling thick and fast,
On the ground my angel left.

The stars are shining so bright now,
Just like they always will,
But you and me we cannot be,
'Cause you've left me lying here.

Lauren Deakin (14)

Health

Reach side to side and do the twirl,
Get on your feet to do a swirl.
Up and down, spin on the floor,
It's about your health and nothing more.

Jumping and running all the time,
Drinking healthy liquids like strawberries and lime.
Swimming this way and that with just a splash,
Skipping down the road as quick as a flash.

Reach side to side and do the twirl,
Get on your feet to do a swirl.
Up and down, spin on the floor,
It's about your health and nothing more.

A bat and a ball will get you fit,
You'll look fashionable in a football kit.
Handstands and cartwheels taking a spin,
Work hard, practise and you will win.

Reach side to side and do the twirl,
Get on your feet to do a swirl.
Up and down, spin on the floor,
It's about your health and nothing more.

Abbie Hull (11)

Heart's Beating Fast, I Just Don't Know Whether It Will Last

We're afraid to go too fast,
Because we don't wanna waste our hearts.
For saying 'I love you' too soon,
Could shortly turn to 'I hate you'.
And then who knows what to do?

We both know that replacement hurts more . . .
Than a b
      r
       o
       k
      e
      n
       heart.
So let's hope we're never gonna be apart.
But it's good to know that all those moments I spent missing you
Just weren't meant to go to waste,
Because if we rushed now
It would all be for nothing
And leave me with a bitter after-taste.

Jenny Csecs (16)

The Train That Never Comes

Standing on a crowded platform just waiting for this train
my ears are cold and I'm in so much pain
Just wanna go home
been busy all day and sit back and relax.
People stare and wait all day but this train will never come
it's been delayed for days.
There's nothing I could do to get this train to hurry,
I just wanna get home and see my family,
but this train will never come,
because my family have gone.

Gemma Fidler (14)

260

Wear My Smile Tonight

I feel like drowning but the tide's too low
I feel like running but I can't let go.
The world has spat me out and I'm in tow
My soul has dried and this life had lied.

Don't worry, it's gonna be alright
I'm gonna wear my smile tonight
Don't worry, it's gonna be alright
I'm gonna wear my smile tonight.

Times have changed and yet the sun still shines
You would have thought it might have drawn the line.
What's the point of lighting a world of crime?
Our world destroyed and running out of time.

Don't worry, it's gonna be alright
I'm gonna wear my smile tonight
Don't worry, it's gonna be alright
I'm gonna wear my smile tonight
Don't worry, it's gonna be alright
I'm gonna wear my smile tonight
Don't worry, it's gonna be alright
I'm gonna wear my smile tonight.

Lewis Theo Clark (16)

Untitled

Don't you know
Don't you know
That my heart can't stop beating?
Can't you see
Can't you see
It was wrong to leave me be?
I know I'm not your perfect girl
And I know I cannot rock your world
But somehow I still believe
We were meant to be.

Jessica Eastell (15)

Lose VS Lose

There's no way you can win,
When love has turned to sin.
When close becomes too close,
When never, is almost.

There's no way to hide,
When it shows on the outside.
When letting go, is letting down,
When being loved, is being drowned.

There's no way,
To rewind what you do.
When what's been done,
Is what defines you.
And then the guilt,
Came and laid you to waste,
Pressed its mouth to yours
And left a bitter taste.

There's no way to choose,
When either way you lose,
When the solution is the problem,
When a decision is the wrong one.

Laura Roberts (15)

I Knew

I knew a girl that could knock you dead
on your feet just by saying hi.
She'd look at you and in two days she'd
have your heart and you'd have hers.
She'd take it, and get to know it then
just leave in a flash.

The writing's on your wall
The empty faces I walk past, I don't belong
My emotional wreckage breaks me down
crashing through steel doors.

I knew a place that could knock you
dead on your feet after just one glimpse.
We'd go there, and we'd never leave
She can't forget it and neither can you.
I'd do it all and get to know it all
Then just leave in a flash.

The writing's on your wall
The empty faces I walk past, I don't belong
My emotional wreckage breaks me down
crashing through steel doors.

Dillon Zhou (16)

You're So . . .

In the race against time we all know who will win
But still, you and I
Run as fast as we can
As days pass us by, I think it all through
And it makes me wonder why

While you . . .
Get lost in your own head,
Eyes open while you sleep in your own bed
You're so, you're soooo
I can't explain it, I can't explain it

Over rooftops, through alleyways
The night is falling on these precious days
You're letting me fall

While you . . .
Get lost in your own head
Eyes open while you sleep in your own bed
You're so, you're soooo
Lost in your own head
Eyes open, eyes open while you sleep in your own bed
You're so, you're so . . .

Molly Highmore (12)

The World

I watched TV just today,
I saw a girl with scars on her face,
She shook in fear as the Earth moved.
The clothes she wore were tattered and torn,
She even wished she was never born,
Is this the world that God first created?

God created, God created, God created, God we pray.

Her mother went to get some food,
Even though it was miles away.
Her daddy was too busy fighting in the war.
Her baby brother shivered and stared,
No cloth or clothes anywhere
And wondering if her mother will return.

Will return, will return, will return, please return.

This song was written for the world,
Even though it's twisted and burnt,
We are still one whole family.

One family, whole family, one family,
Even though we don't all know!

Rachael Egan (13)

Untitled

What an awkward creature, I behold!
Two brows knitted determinedly,
Fiercely resolute on his antipathy.
A man who shuns all society,
Without consequence.

Oh, my sweet misanthropist,
Why must you afflict me so?
Retreating jealously into yourself,
Only to deny me your light, your love . . .

La la l'amour . . .

How cruel he scowls upon the world!
Yet I spy, behind this stony countenance,
An atypical beauty lies dormant,
Haughty angel, wake!

Oh, my sweet misanthropist,
Why must you afflict me so?
Retreating jealously into yourself,
Only to deny me your light, your love . . .

La la l'amour . . .

Rebecca Myers (17)

You Are The Girl For Me

Yes you are
Because I love when you
Laugh at my jokes
You make me smile every time I see you
When you knock on my door I'm always dressed just for you
When I'm scared you always
Cuddle me and say it is OK
I love you being there for me
I just love you.

Lucy Holland (13)

Shoot Straight To The Top

Before things used to be as good,
But that was then and things start to change.
Do not leave things for tomorrow,
Cos if you do, nothing will be completed.
Take me just right to that part,
When I used to be a good girl,
How could I land to that start
Where the goodness used to be?
Every day there's a chance for you to raise that bar,
But you throw it all away and it won't get you that far.
You know it won't shoot you straight to the top,
You know it won't shoot you straight to the top.
And I've experienced before and now I find it as a chore,
Cos I know that the future would be something that I adore,
You know it will shoot you straight to the top,
You know it will shoot you straight to the top.
The world could be a tougher place,
With people persuading,
Telling you to change,
But if you've got a stronger willpower,
It will just hit you and feel like nothing happened.

Brooke Johnson (12)

Away I Go

I start packing my case
I am so excited
The look on my face
Where will I go?
India, Australia, America, no!
Spain, a place with beaches, hotels and sun
I cannot wait, it is going to be such fun

Then I fly away
Off I go less than a day
What shall I do when I arrive?

Charlotte Presley (13)

Treasure It Forever!

If you look into my eyes
What will you see?
A girl that cries
For you baby!
I don't wanna lose you
But I can't keep on!
This feeling is true
Baby I love you,
Baby we were meant to be,
You can't deny
Everyone can see
I love you baby.
Say you don't care
And tell a lie
My heart may tear,
But that's alright
I know you feel the same
Everyone can tell
Love ain't just a stupid game,
It's something you should treasure!
Not now, but forever!

Emily Perry (14)

The War Of Love/The Love Of War

We were fighting again.
That time I don't know how it started.
Neither was stopping,
'cause both of us simply refused to.
Then we were having a war of words,
words hurting much more,
more harsh and painful,
than even bullets could be
and what makes it worse,
is that we both enjoyed hurting the other's feelings.
It was all because of you;
I knew your heart was with them, not me.
Wasn't I good enough for you on my own?
Our love was part
of your harsh, pretend hurtful show.
That's not the way relationships should go.
Why couldn't you stick with just one?
It broke my heart in two,
so I had to leave you
And you seemed happy too.
So why do I regret it now?

Joanna Channon (14)

Looking At The World

People look at the world
Tell me now
Can you see it there
Tell me how?

People see the low side
Of most things
But they don't keep an open mind
About most things

'Cause they don't know
And they don't care
They live a life of lies
Like a web

They weave and stitch and sew
But they just don't know
What's going on in the world
Right now

Let's create another world
A better place
A cooler sound.

Michelle Watson (12)

Star

I was walking alone in the dark
Just like any other day.

Chorus
Because you're a shining star
Who lights the darkness
Giving warmth to the cold
And brightening my day.

And you came up and said hello
Suddenly all my worries were lifted
When I met you.

Chorus
You said you'd call me later
And I went home
Sat by the phone.

Chorus
It got late
You still hadn't called me
I grew tired of you
And you're not my star anymore.

Rebecca Tweed (12)

My Song To You

Chorus
It's so hard; it's so hard to write this song to you,
Writing the words but nothing is clear.

Verse 1
I am lost, lost without the ideas and I'm thinking what's next.
I had my ideas in my head, in my head and I thought of this.
The words I was thinking were the words to my song,
I hummed them in my head and tapped the rhythm on my drums.

Chorus
It's so hard; it's so hard to write this song to you,
Writing the words but nothing is clear.

Verse 2
The clock was ticking as I was writing this song,
The ideas kept rolling around in my mind.
Finally, at last the words came to my head,
I put the words to paper and sang the tune in my head.

Chorus
It's so hard; it's so hard to write this song to you,
Writing the words but nothing is clear.

Bradley Wool (12)

If I Could ...

If I could do anything,
I would rule the world,
What if I did it?
Does that sound absurd?

If I could be anyone,
Anyone but me,
Would you let me do it?
Let me be?

If I could have anything,
I would change the Earth,
Can I make it more happy?
Bring in more love?

If I could do something,
What would I do?
Live so happily?
But for who?

I know that I can change the Earth,
Let me do it!
It's not absurd!

Salma Riaz (13)

Martyr

Kiss me in the city of hallows
Let me dream till I break
Love me, leave me, lose me
With the heart you'll take
Watch me die without the anger
Before the sepia memories fade
When time has frozen over
On a loveless crusade
Pretend, you be the liar
Build me then let me break
And let me perish in the name of love
For nothing but your sake

It's a diabolical rat race
The way I fly before I fall
That endless vicious circle
That makes me feel so small
It's a diabolical rat race
The way I fly before I fall
They say it's better to have loved and lost
But I'd rather never have loved at all.

Shannon Britton (14)

Untitled

I to the C to the E to the CREAM
If you have a try then
You'll see what I mean
Jump to the left
Jump to the right
We'll be eating ice cream all night
Eating McFlurry, you can't say sorry
It's the plan of today
Everyone you know is gonna come this way
The plan for today is ice cream all day
Hey!

Christopher Akpokodje (12)

Breathe

I see you watching me
Come over here and talk to me
We'll talk sometime and get closer
Then you expect me to give you my number
Just breathe, breathe
Why do all these boys expect so much?
I'm just a girl, is that not enough?
I need a minute, just leave me alone
They think I'm easy but they don't know
Just breathe, breathe
I'm a supergirl and I'll never get hurt
Baby you can't touch me
But you slowly find a way up into my heart
And secretly you crush me
Just breathe, breathe
The pattern repeats over again
Again, again, again
I see you watching me
Come over here
And talk to me.

Bethany Tyler (13)

Strings Of The Heart

Are you calling me
Are you trying to get through?
I thought we were over
Cos I'm over you
You said that you loved me,
But these words weren't true.
I've opened so many doors in my heart
To let you through.
You've hurt me so much
That words can't undo.
But that's just me and you.

Emily Purchase (13)

Easy Peasy

I've worked it out,
It didn't take much,
I've known him so long,
But we still could not touch.
I wanted him,
I fancy him so,
He won't look at me,
He wouldn't even dance.
Now what to do,
Can't take it no more,
Stop messin' me around,
It is just so stupid.
Can't hold them back,
Hold my tears back,
My hopes all intact,
I just had to split up.
It was easy,
So lemon squeezy,
Cos there was no love,
His love was with others.

Georgia Naughton (12)

Love Is Enough

Love is enough, it's a lifetime of training,
But the world has no voice but the voice of complaining,
Love is enough, it's special to discover,
But there's a difference between love and finding a lover,
Love is enough, through the paths unknown,
No one should go through life unloved and alone,
Love is enough, without race or creed,
It ignores all the evils; hate, disease and greed,
Love is enough, it acts as a muse,
A painting, a poem, that only you can choose,
Love is enough, to die for and live for.

Claire Sycamore (17)

Dreaming

I have been searching for my dream all my life,
But looking in the wrong places,
And it has always caused me trouble and strife,
Because I always find the wrong faces,
In my head I have this imaginary world,
It is like a fairy tale and,
All I want is for this world to be unfurled,
But this life always seems to fail,
I want to be appreciated or my heart might break,
I want to show the world just who I am,
I want to be noticed by the world for whatever it may take,
That is what I am dreaming, that's my plan,
In this magical fairy tale of my own,
I am always the shining star,
I live like a princess with a golden crown,
I have a big stretch limo car,
In my dream world everything is all about me,
If it came true I'd be beaming,
I don't have to be troubled as you can see,
But I'm dreaming, dreaming, dreaming.

Caitlin Greenshields (13)

Untitled

The silence is so loud, it's treating you with fear
You think he's around the corner
You're certain he's gonna be here
Buy reality he doesn't know who you are
Reality ... you're not a star
Reality ... he ain't gonna walk through your back door
Reality ... you're Cinderella and you're poor
Reality ... Cindy, you better get back to scrubbing them floors
coz he ain't taking you to the ball!
Stop this fantasy and dreaming
You need to get your act together and start cleaning.

Tayba Imran (15)

Secrets

The day has come for me to tell,
All of the things I hide so well,
See all of you haters just don't understand,
All I need is someone to hold my hand,
I wish I could show you all of my secrets,
But if I tell them or expose my weakness,
Then you could see,
You could easily break and tear through me.
I need a hand to guide my way,
To help me through the path that's lay,
And I pray every night,
Because you're all I have in this life.
Seeing you, it makes me strong,
And you give me the strength to carry on.
See, for peace in the world I'm a big supporter,
All these kids want to drink is water,
And you have no love because you never received it,
And that's because you didn't teach it.
So teach this, just let the kids go,
Because love is an emotion trapped in your soul.

Jasmine Hextall (13)

Hidden Warrior

Tug on my heartstrings
What do you see?
'Cause I see the ghost
Of a far out memory.
A haunted figure
Silhouetted across the moon,
Distance may seem difficult
But I promise, I'll be with you soon.
Shut your eyes a moment
Stay here in my arms,
I'll sing you to sleep
Protect you from harm.
Just grit your teeth
Choke back your tears,
I know you're a warrior
So fight away your fears.
I'll catch you if you fall
Don't let this fade away
You ask me to save you?
Darling, any day.

Georgia Goulding (14)

One And Only

You're always there when I need you
I love you so much,
you're my one and only.
I love you and you love me
that's why,
you're my one and only.
When I have troubles or I am upset
you're there through it all,
you're my one and only.
I love you and you love me
that's why,
you're my one and only.
I never wanna lose you
I love you,
you're my one and only.
I love you and you love me
that's why
you're my one and only
Yh, yh, yh
one and only.

Sherrie Barrios (12)

Lovin' Afta Hurtin'

The flowers are bloomin'
And the birds are hummin'
It's a beautiful summer's day
But not for me

The sky feels black
And the clouds are grey
Instead of rays of sunlight
It's raining today
And it's all because of you

You made me hurt
You made me cry
You stopped me as the world passed by
But now I don't know why
I still feel like this now you're gone
I still feel sad
It's stupid, it's wrong
It's silly, it's bad
I must be mad
But somehow I still love you.

Vicky Bailey (13)

In Love With Another

I've got a new look, I've got a new you,
Straighten your face while I straighten my hair,
I was all yours till you messed up my life,
Now whatever you say I don't care.

Because you and me together,
We just ain't right for each other,
'Cause I'm in love,
I'm in love,
I'm in love with another.

There I stood, in the pouring rain,
Shouting at you, but we were miles apart,
I'd have still been here with you,
If you hadn't gone and broken my heart.

Because you and me together,
We just ain't right for each other,
'Cause you're in love,
You're in love,
You're in love with another.

Holly Campbell (12)

Street Of Dreams

And as long as this road seems,
I know it's called the street of dreams,
But all my dreams do is fade,
Like a stupid serenade.
From dreaming there's nothing to gain,
Nothing fictitious ever remains.
And if the truth be known, my love,
You are all I'm dreaming of.
Yes, the words they are old,
But the meaning is new,
Like my reason for being,
That reason is you.

Thomas Radcliffe (15)

21st Century Life

Look at you; look at me, worrying about the strife
But hey! This is what happens in 21st century life.
You worry about the bus fares, you worry about the time
You get charged adult prices, when it shouldn't cost a dime.
They associate us with knife crime, they think of us as yobs
They encourage us to work, but they never give us jobs.
They don't take the time to know us,
they judge by what they're told
They read it in the newspaper which every day they're sold.
I'd like to tell them different, but would they listen? No!
There's no point trying to be friendly if they think that I'm a foe.
The tabloids think they know it all, with knife crime on the climb
But really, they have no idea what's going through our minds.
They think that we're obsessed with those little things called drugs
And assume that every teenager is a mugger or a thug.
They don't realise it yet, but the people like you and me
We deserve a respected place in this society.
Look at you; look at me, worrying about the strife
But hey! This is what happens in 21st century life.

Libby Maddocks (14)

Animals

When the sun don't shine anymore
Monkeys, baboons and galore
they will play the whole night long
singing songs never sung
the streets are full with the zoo
it's an animal party for me and you
so let's party back into the night
don't you worry, I never do bite
snakes and divas surrounding me
but I won't let go that easily
you're a very rare specimen
I don't want to stay friends.

Anil Patel (17)

Sun-Sense

Di weather is so hot it lick yuh pon your neck back.
It drain out all di salt,
So yuh need a Supermalt
And a Dragon Stout fi put back the liquid
The sun nyam out.
In di future, don't stand out in di sun
And allow yuh skin fi bun.
Instead, fling on di sunlotion
In the right proportion . . .
Drink plenty of wata, dash in some ice
Suh it keep yuh feelin' cool and nice
Lay dung in di shade while the other idiots sunbathe
And mek dem skin fade.
So stick to dese rules and don't play the fool
Memba, always stay cool.
Forget the nonsense,
Learn some
Sun-sense!
Peace and love.

Shoshana Espeut (17)

Shooting Star Hospice

People, people hear me out,
Listen to me without a doubt,
Shooting Star has come so far, so hear me out right now.
Children dying tonight whilst their adults are crying.
Donate, donate, donate
If you don't hate, so give us a hand and be a mate,
Shooting star has come so far
People, people hear me now, we need to save over sideways and under,
We can save them right now
Shooting Star, a dazzling star that shines so bright
We have come to an end.
Thanks for your lend so this is the Shooting Star Hospice.

Marisa Harman (13)

Friendship

You're a true friend,
I thought you should know.
The kindness of you,
Helped our friendship grow.
We've been through some tough times,
But we've made it through.
The best friend that I've ever known was you.
When life gets you down,
I'll always be there.
I hope it will help you,
I will always care.
We have a special bond,
That I hope will not break.
You make me as happy
As a freshly baked cake.
You supported me always when I was in tears,
We stuck together as we conquered our fears.
Sometimes we fight but I know that it's wrong,
That's why I decided to write you this song.

Erin Menzies (13)

The World Is Our Future

We are the children
We are the future
We bring the world closer together
There should be no more fighting
There should be no more wars
or there will be no future for us all
so let the children unite
and to bring the world as one because
We are the children
We are the future
We bring the world closer together
We bring the world together as one.

Maria Kelleher (14)

Rainbow

As the bright coloured, shiny stripes,
Shine in the long dark starry distance,
They reflect off the big white dashing moon,
Letting off tiny sparkles which luminously shine through space and dazzle right
through every planet.

Glowing and changing colour.
Always making dreams come true
as it watches fiercely through the night dazzling sky.
Big, bold colours, every colour you could dream of,
and every colour has a meaning.
Purple means joy and happiness,
Red means love,
Yellow means the bright hot sun,
and green means the long spiky grass,
that sprouts up from the ground.
Every colour combines together, to make one massive beautiful rainbow.
The colours never die down,
They just simply blossom all the way through the night
Until day time appears and then it magically disappears.

Leanne Drain (15)

Special Things

Where the mud is brown,
And the grass is green,
And I ate a big can of beans,
There was a lady called Sarah,
In a big, red house with a small, yellow car,
Out in the drive,
With a little, little duck,
And a little, little boot,
With the monkey,
And a bee, with a pineapple tree,
So sing along with me,
Woo, woo, oh yeh!

Ellie Bicknell (8)

Being In Love With You

Standing here
With a shield of fear
Hoping one day
You'll come my way
Wishing I will see you around
Maybe down the town
Should have listened to what trouble said
You have a heart of lead
I cried all night long
Then I wrote this song
Should have run away awfully far
Or perhaps stolen a car
Anywhere away from you
So I wouldn't feel so blue
It will never be the same
Please don't take the blame
My heart is broken
Though you're standing there smoking
But I'm still in love with you.

Beth Macpherson (13)

A Special World

A special world for you and me
A special bond one cannot see
It wraps us up in a cocoon
And holds us fiercely in its womb
Its fingers spread like fine spun gold
Gently nestling us to the fold
Like silken thread it holds us fast
Bonds like this are meant to last
And though times a thread may break
A new one forms in its wake
To bind us closer and keep us strong
In a special world where we belong.

Chelsea Robson (14)

Change

Every night you make me feel so happy and relaxed.
When you go home you leave me in such a mess
the very next day you're ringing me up saying let's do it again
I need to change and so do you
but how, ooh, how do we both change?
Yeah, how do we both change?
How can we carry on doing this
I've gotta worry about more important things in my life
like staying alive and healthy
I don't know how to put this, but I'm leaving you
I don't want anything to do with you
you betta leave my life right now
I didn't want to do that, but it's the best thing to do for us
we've gotta change
yeah change
change our lives to be better, ooh
change
change
change, ooh, yeah, change.

Elizabeth Robson (13)

My Farm

Once upon a time there was a silly farmer,
Who had ducks, sheep, hens and five hairy llamas.
Lena, Lana, Lara and Linde were the girls
And eat was all they did,
The only boy was Leo,
But we called him smashed up Sid.
One chicken's name was Becky, the other Ermintrude,
And all they did was cluck and lay
And steal each other's food.
Plenty of sheep are in the field as far as we can see,
But all they do is eat the grass
And baa and poo and wee.

Zahra Longdon (9)

288

My Song For You

You're so far away, millions and millions of miles,
You make my life shine, you make me smile.
You're the only thing on my mind,
You're the one I believe in to make hard days okay,
Maybe one day you'll be so much more
Than my faith, hope and my life,
But that's the furthest anything can go.
Maybe no one knows, but I hope you do,
That I love you.
You'll never have to leave my heart,
No matter how far apart.
My dreams are about you,
My senses detect you.
Anything maybe can be in our way,
But nothing can be between our hearts.
The dark may be scary,
But thinking of you makes me so much better.
It's time to say goodbye now,
But not forever.

Hollie Camilleri (13)

Figuring Out

Figuring out what's going to happen next,
not knowing where to turn to.
Trying hard to concentrate
but the pain still hurts
wanting to see you again
writing letters again and again
thinking about the times we had
All the good and all the bad
thinking about what could have been
but it didn't turn out how I thought it would seem.
Figuring out what's going to happen next.

Milly Mintram (12)

The Secret Society

Is this the beginning
Of a world with no means to an end?
We can't hide from every decision
Yes, we have a life to mend.

Let's break this fixation
What are we fighting for?
This broken dictation
Unwind and open your mind.

See the future unfold
Hear the secrets untold
And follow my lead, into a world where we can be free.

We can't live forever
But we can play the game
We'll sneak away to our secret society
To show the world we're not the same.

Hand in hand, they will understand
As we slowly fade away.

Kirsty Davison (15)

I Love Birds

Going on an adventure
Somewhere in the world
I don't know where.

Looking for birds
Any birds
Parrots with bright feathers
Penguins eating fish
Owls hooting at night
In the morning the robin sings.

I wish
Birds would sing with me
Sitting in the tree.

Find a baby bird
Feed it a worm.

I like birds
They fly a long, long way
Up there in the sky.

Lorna Freestone (12)

Get Me Out Of Here!

When I walk into the darkness and I feel the wind a-blow,
Children playing in my head, I walk this road alone.
Trees swaying side to side, quietness everywhere.
Please get me out of here, I'm really, really scared.

Chorus
Get me out of here, I need help.
I'm being chased by something else.
Someone please help me out before it gets so much worse.

Now I'm not so scared alone,
Someone's here to help me through and face my strange fear.
Someone's with me all the way, counting my steps.
Two hearts beat at once as we walk through the air.
Please get me out of here, I'm really, really scared.

Chorus
Get me out of here, I need help.
I'm being chased by something else.
Someone please help me out before it gets so much worse.

Abbie Hayday (12)

The Spirit Of Fun

There's a spirit inside me waiting to get out,
And when it does I will scream and shout,
But this spirit is no ordinary one,
It's a spirit that makes me want to have fun!
Whatever the weather, night or day,
I just want to go out with my friends and play,
Ride on your bikes, maybe go to the pool,
Anything that makes us look really cool,
It's the beginning of the new week back at school,
With all the teachers that are so very cruel,
My spirit is raging trying to get out,
But come the bell for home time,
It will scream and shout.

Jason Lang (13)

The Sheffield United Song

I'm watching the blades in my shades,
Killgallon has just scored,
The Palace fans look bored,
I think that today is the day,
It was definitely worth 10 pounds pay,

Four nil, up thrashing United,
Surely the keeper must be short-sighted,
Eating my chip butty,
While the fans are going nutty,

United, you blew me away,
Fans are singing,
Blades are winning,
No one is chinning hooray!

Cotterill running down the wing,
The Palace fans don't know how to sing,
Bramall Lane is going insane,
Palace are just playing lame.

Joe Fox (11)

Don't Fight!

I don't know what to do
I've been thinkin' of you
I've been thinkin'
What would happen if you went to fight
All I've got to say
Is please don't fight
I'm beggin' you, don't fight
I'll do anythin', please don't fight
I'll do anythin', you'll like
You're my destiny
I've shared most of my dreams
Dreamin' 'bout you
I can't stop dreamin', thinkin' 'bout you.

Yahya Mohammed (12)

You're More Than Everything

You were my beautiful dream
That kept me asleep
Now you're an ugly nightmare
That kept me up all night
The way you could instantly make me smile was amazing
Now all you do is make me cry
I adored the way you gazed at me
But now it just makes me feel uncomfortable
I thought you were my first true love
So I guess love is something I will never get
I thought you were there for me when I was sad
But your hugs don't make it better anymore
I remember the first time I was with you and your friends
But now they all hate me and glare
Most of all I hate the reason I still love you
Because the truth is I miss you
And you are *all* I ever need
I love you.

Lauren Freeman (12)

Pets!

I've got lots of pets and they are all hungry.
I've got two greedy rabbits,
I've got 14 birds, 2 cockatiels the size of someone's head,
I've got a hamster (who can fit New York in his pouch).

There's so much animal food in the house,
It's like a pet shop!

Feeding them is really hard,
I use a bag as big as my sister a day.

I've got lots of pets and they are all hungry.
I've got two greedy rabbits,
I've got 14 birds, 2 cockatiels the size of someone's head,
I've got a hamster (who can fit New York in his pouch).

Garrad Willson (11)

Abandoned

'Save me', I scream to the hole in my heart,
For this is the pain I wish to part,
My delicate, glass heart has been smashed,
But even when repaired you can still see the crack,
Darling, I need you,
Lord knows, I need you,
When I'm with you I feel exhilarated and alive,
Without you I feel all entity has died,
Tell me how you could leave me like this,
You'll always know how deeply your love is missed,
Darling, I need you
Lord knows, I need you
Why do you pretend what we had never existed,
When love was all our lives consisted?
Now I wait here for you to return,
For it's purely your love that I yearn
Darling, I need you,
Lord knows, I need you.

Hannah Pilley Rabbs (14)

Fairy Tale Disaster

You make everything disappear
So it's just you and me
But I'm living in a fairy tale
You want her, I can see it in your eyes
I'm just a big dreamer
Wasting my time in a fairy tale
Snow White and Cinderella are my best friends
The big bad wolf huffs and puffs
I just wish you could be my knight in shining armour
Come and save me from this nightmare
Be a true prince charming
But I'm destined to loneliness
Trapped in a fairy tale.

Hannah Ritchie (13)

Waiting Alone

Walking on a cold beach
walking near the ocean
the one that pulls your cold
feet away from the beach.
Picking up the cold sand
letting it run through my hand
waiting for that day
where I can command, where I can command.
Waiting, waiting is frustrating
standing here on my own, waiting
for that special day, for that special day to come along
to come along.
Hey, hey everybody look and stare
I'm all alone but I don't care.
No, I don't care, no, no.
Hey, hey everybody look, look, look and stare
I'm alone, but I don't really care, no, no
I don't really care.

Charlie Bennett (12)

Forgotten People

Pay some attention,
and open your eyes,
take a good look around,
it may be a surprise.
I don't want to shock or scare,
just need to make you aware.
Do you care at all,
about what goes on,
those forgotten people,
crying their unheard song?
I don't want to shock or scare,
just need to make you aware.
Go, take some time out
your busy schedule,
just stop for a minute,
think about those people,
starved, held hostage, abducted,
trafficked, threatened and beaten.

Jasmine Poxon (13)

Untitled

I look in the mirror
And don't recognise
The face that's staring back
Or the stranger's eyes

The mask that I wear
(I never take it off)
Shows the fake one, the lie
The girl they all know

Dreading every day and what might come my way
I wake up and remember who I have to be
And as I walk away, my peers sigh and say
'Who was that?', 'I don't know her,' 'I feel so betrayed'.
Shedding tears, every night
Is this wrong, or is this right?
I don't know who I should be
Should I be her
Or should I be me?

Katie Gardner-Edwards (13)

You And Me

On the streets of London
People walk all day
Doing all the things they wanna do
Without a care in the world
But what do the homeless do?

Where do all the people go
At the end of the day?
Where do all the people go
When it's cold and grey?
Where do you and I go
When we are lost?
Where do the homeless go
When they need a break?

The streets are never empty
There's always someone there
Where does everyone go
At the end of the day?

Michelle Sharpe (12)

Music

Music is a great thing to me,
It makes me and you feel happy,
Don't matter if it's fast or slow,
As long as the lyrics have a flow,
Many blast it aloud,
but others prefer to sing in crowds.

R 'n' B so sweet to me,
MC Rhymes are signs to me,
Being an artist lets you express yourself,
The same with music without a doubt,
Tunes and melodies influence,
They make you resent violence,
Lyrics tell you something with a hidden message or a code,
Music can help to lighten the load.

Every year, month, week and day
music lives on,
It will never die to I, Tom.

Thomas Cummings-Sammons (12)

The Crows On The Moor

We are the crows that fly in the sky,
We are the crows so mysterious and black,
We fly through the night like a witch on her broom.

We are clouded in fear, so mysterious are we,
Black magic we use to strike fear into you,
Dark sorcerers are we hiding in plain sight.

A thousand knives are we, waiting to attack,
A flock or a murder is what we are called,
One beady eye, not two, not three,
Watching, always watching.

I sit on a wall and watch the crows fly away,
The crows are crafty, planning their way,
But I know that the crows are peaceful inside,
At the end of the day.

Yes the crows are peaceful,
The crows on the moor ...

Alison Russo (12)

I Know

I know you're always there for me
Well I'm always there for you
I always wonder where you've gone
And I worry about what you do

Don't let go of your memories
Never push me aside
Someday soon we'll escape together
And float away with the tide

I never thought you'd ever go
Just escape without me
Your heart's whole – mine's split in two
You may be fine but I'll never be

I know you're always there for me
Though I'm not there for you
I don't care where you've gone
And I don't care what you do.

Ayesha Chouglay (14)

Too Good For Me

Have you ever loved someone who was too good for you?
But deep down you knew,
That your love was true!
She would smile at you
And hold your hand,
But you and here knew that
She was for another man.
Because you were Buttons
And she was Cinderella,
And all you wanted to do
Was to hold her umbrella.
You wanted to protect her,
So finally you and her,
Would be . . . to-ge-th-er!

Jake Manning (13)

Disguise

Alone I sit,
Sad, just a bit,
I think about yesterday,
And wonder if I'll be OK.

This place feels so wrong,
I feel I don't belong,
But the only thing I fear,
Is that you won't be here.

I want you to be here with me,
Even though you're not,
They tell me to forget,
But I miss you a lot.

I'm sick of all this laughter,
I'm sick of all these lies,
Nobody will understand,
The things that I disguise.

Hannah Fretton (14)

My Inspiration

When I first saw you,
You were out of my league,
Then I saw you again,
And you looked normal to me,
Then I realised,
You're the one I'm looking for,
The one I need,
When I needed inspiration,
You took my hand in yours,
And then I felt this click between us two,
All of a sudden, I'm floating in mid air,
Little did I know I found the one,
So now I realised,
You're my inspiration.

Sophie Hancock (13)

My Friend

I look into your eyes and see your peace
our bond is strong
we ride together
with a sense of release

You are my friend
who never judges me
I am your friend
and will always be

Together we achieve goals
we work as a team
jumping over poles
and across the stream

You are my friend
who never judges me
you are my horse
and forever will be.

Laura Chandler (12)

Who You Are Is Me

Verse
When the time is right,
I know that we should fight for our lives,
When the time is right,
Everything will be alright.

Chorus
We've got nothing to say,
We've got nothing to do,
We've got nothing, nothing to play.

Who you are is perfect,
Who you are is me,
Who you are is me and you together,
(Forever!) x 2.

Shona Havard (12)

Let's Make A Start

Longing for water,
They're going to die.
Help the children,
Before their wings fly.

Winter is near now,
Let's make a start.
Do what you can,
Play your best part.

Give them some love,
Something to eat.
A toy or shelter,
Or even some sheets.

They need our love,
They need our hearts.
Keep them alive,
Let's make a start.

Lancy Miranda (14)

The Fight

Up down, left right
Let's go and pick a fight
No, no one cares about me
All I want is a family

Don't know where to go
Don't know who I ought to know
Don't know where to sleep
Don't think I can even eat

Chorus:
Don't know, I don't know
Where to go when it's throwing it down with snow,
Horrible people in the street that I don't really want to meet.
Not very nice, they bully you for a price.

Andrew Kelly (11)

The Summer Rain

Side by side, we walked
Our fragile words lost in the downpour
Fat drops burst upon your cheeks, your hair,
I envy them their touch
And now I see loving you is worth this pain
As you walk me through the summer rain

Careworn traveller, warm as you brush
My hand, I swear I still feel that touch
Reminding me that you are real
The rain taps out the rhythm I feel

He said the rain made him feel alive
And I see it, sparkling in azure eyes
Drops resonate off him and onto my cheek
I swear I never saw a smile so sweet

Tonight, being with you, could bring me no shame
Walking with you in the summer rain.

Sophie Phillips (15)

Christmas Is On The Horizon

Christmas is on the horizon
Christmas is coming soon
so we'll keep on going 'till
the snow comes down on you.

Where the snow falls upon tree tops
Santa's packing too
with Christmas on the horizon
he'll be here soon.

There's snow flakes
and Christmas cakes
cards from me to you
so let's all be good cos
Mr Robin's watching you.

Emily Hardy-Trodd (13)

306

Nothing

Look at me, in my room
Doing nothing, in the gloom
Nowt to do. Nowt to say
If anyone comes I shout, 'Go away.'

I'm doing nothing
Nothing is fun
Fun is nothing
Nothing is fun.

Look at me in my room
Doing nothing in the gloom
Nowt to do. Nowt to say
If anyone comes I shout, 'Go away.'

I've changed my mind
Nothing is boring
Boring is nothing
Let's go outside.

Jack Bailey (10)

Trust

Everyone got somebody they can trust
But what do you do when you know you must
Leave 'em, they take your money, leave you bust
It's like iron, hmm, leave 'em and they rust.

Three paths to take, one can copy me
Take the other, leave you penny free
Third, take drugs, not ma cup of tea
Live life, be smart, be free.

Drinking is something that you shouldn't do
If you do, try to think it through
It would really just make you
Absolutely play the fool.

Kyle McInnes Hunter (14)

Unhappy Ending

Every time I look at you,
My heart breaks - splits in two,
When will I ever learn,
That everything I touch burns?

The same has happened yet again,
With you, will this cycle never end?
You'd be better off without me.

Like the others,
Cower in shame,
'Cause you daren't speak my name,
With anything like affection,
'Cause you know you'll have an unhappy ending.

Like me, then you'll be cursed,
To know that what you love will burn,
Knowing you can't reverse these changes,
Knowing you'll have an unhappy ending.

Alice Pepper (15)

A Place Where I Belong

Don't know what I've done to get here,
Don't know what I've done wrong,
All I need is a little love,
And a place where I belong.

No one bothers to help me,
No one really cares,
People have been told about it,
So when they see me, they stop and stare.

I wish someone would say 'I'll help you,
And make it go away',
But today's not my turn,
Maybe another old day.

I don't know what I've done that was so bad,
Don't know what I've done to get this.
All I want in life is to talk to someone
And in the end get a cuddle and a night-time kiss.

Sarah Moore (14)

Broken Hearted

Baby, you did me wrong,
I thought your love for me was strong,
But obviously it's not,
What was the point of tying our knot?
No longer gonna waste my breath,
I'm gonna get out of this mess.
You're not my Mr Right
And I'm no longer your wife.
That's why I'm getting on this flight.
So say bye-bye to me
And give me your house key,
You're no longer in our bed
Because you're messing with my head.
So stop playing games with me,
I'm going to say bye-bye baby,
Bye-bye baby,
Baby.

Shannon Jones (13)

The Blue Beat

The bombs are dropping, they're exploding,
Guns are firing and people running.
So much noise, it's so contagious,
Can't stay longer, it's so dangerous.

So much annoyance, I can't take it,
Must slow down or I won't make it,
Gonna kill someone to make the peace,
But I can't do it, I can't hold on any more.

Instrumental

When it goes dark, it's so scary,
You can hear them listening
For the sign of a victim,
But they will never catch me!

Jack Jermy-Doyle (13)

Inspired

Coming at me, chasing all over the town,
Ready for me,
My heart's beating faster now
Picking pieces, heart's achieving a broken smile
Love is needed, we're gonna pump it up a while
Dreaming the night, dreaming away
Baby, I'm sick of this, sick of you
You're telling me that you love is real
It's just weakening me, just like you do
Walking closer, like you've got something to hide
Waiting hours, passion from lovers who lied
Can't help thinking, what's involving my galaxy
It doesn't matter, defences are following me
Staking the prayer, stalking the fire
Coward when stoo, welcomed alone
All along just falling in love with you
By misfortune, my love had turned to stone.

Hannah Walls (12)

This Love

Help me experience love the way I never have before,
Both you and I can paint a fairy tale that lasts forevermore,
We don't need to go too far as long as it's you and me,
For it's you who has stolen my heart and I long to forever be.

We can go to the forest,
Or take a long walk by the beach,
The sunset will surround us, and with a kiss, we'll lose our speech,
The night will come and bring us desire,
For the romance it abides, ignites a blissful fire.

Our hearts filled with passion, will at last intertwine,
It's this love I can't hide, and from hurt I finally resign.

I'll fall in love once again if you promise to be true,
For fate has it, that my heart and destiny, now belong to you.

Gregg Hearn (15)

Look At Me

I love the way you look at me
Your eyes so bright they're all I see
Your smile so warm is all I need
To make me smile, I could walk many a mile,
and still be smiling all the while.
So baby, just look at me, that's all you gotta do
So baby, just look at me, I'll be just enjoyin' the view
So baby, just look at me, 'cause I love lookin' at you
Baby, just look at me, p-lease.
I love the way you look at me
Your hair so perfect, please don't change
I'm happy now, now don't turn the page
Our happy ever after, God I really love her, we're really made for each other.
So baby, just look at me, that's all you gotta do
So baby, just look at me, I'll be just enjoyin' the view
So baby, just look at me, 'cause I love lookin' at you
Baby just look at me p-lease.

Vishal Gossain (13)

One Last Time

As the river flows inside my heart
As the softness of your lips touch my face
As your starry gaze filters my eyes

And the day I stop loving you
Is the day that I will die

And the nights that grew colder
And the days that grew warm
I would see you one last time

And the day I stop loving you
Is the day I will die

And I would see you in Heaven instead
The bright lights that sparkle
In front of my eyes
I would see your smile
One last time.

Byrony McFarlane (14)

Dream On

It started off a dream,
Inside my heart,
Glowing inside of me,
Like a shooting star,
Then I opened up,
Showed what's inside of me,
Look where I am now,
Exactly where I wanna be!

'Cause when you have a dream,
Never hide it,
Just let it rip,
And soon you'll find that
No matter who you are,
No matter what you do,
If you look hard enough,
You'll find a star in you!

Erin Phillips (12)

My Fantasy World

In my fantasy world there would be
Gold at the end of every rainbow
And houses made out of gingerbread
In my fantasy world there would be
Clouds made out of marshmallows
And grass made out of laces
In my fantasy world there would be
Teddy bears that could walk and talk
And a field that grows chocolate
In my fantasy world there would be
A hidden room with all my secrets trapped inside
And have my very own time machine
In my fantasy world
I could live forever
Accompanied by only my friends and family.

Lisa McLachlan (13)

Love Beyond Death

The way she breathes
The way he feels
The way she holds his curse-ed soul
He's just another way to die
Will her kiss still taste this sweet
Once horror's over?
As his demons control her mind
They'll all bow down before them

Blood drips from her eyes
Watching it all fall down
The burning never stops
The pain won't die
Holding her in his dying arms
She's the closest thing to perfection
He won't ever let her go
Make his heartbeat last forever.

Ellie Wilkinson (13)

What To Write?

You can see the words inside your head,
But which ones do you choose?
So many ideas
But which will win, which will lose?
This is a chance in a lifetime,
But whose life? I don't know.
I'm trying so much, working so hard,
Will it show?
To think, to dream, oh what does it mean?
'Writer's block' they call it, it's much more
No ideas, no words
Trying so hard it almost hurts
It makes me think *what am I doing this for?*
For that one chance in a lifetime
What if it's not mine?

Lily Shahmoon (12)

Chains

Sometimes I wish upon a star to wake up where you are
So we can be together . . . forever . . .
And we'd dance among the stars that beautiful night
You won't slip through my fingers this time
And I never wanna wake up from this sleep
I thought you'd stay in my life
But you came and went like the morning breeze
And now you're gone forever . . . forever

Sometimes I feel like I'm breaking free from the pain
But then I think of you and me, and what we could have been
I felt so high, upon our cloud
But the chain around my heart kept pullin' me down.
You being gone makes me feel so alone
There's no one else but you I wanna phone
I just need to hear that sweet voice of yours
How could I ask for anything more?

Lucy Hyams (14)

Death At The Brink Of Sadness
(3rd Wave Ska)

Excuse me, do you know the way to the mystery?
C'mon, I want to see his lonely road
Never thought I'd get to see the day he died
But now he's free of his heavy load
Before he died, he left the parchment on his desk
Said he couldn't wait for his soul to be put to rest
His life was a living so every night he cried
So I saw his body lying there
And I couldn't help but shed a tear
Because everything he learned from life suddenly became clear to me
Before he died, he left the parchment on his desk
Said he couldn't wait for his soul to be put to rest
His life was a living so every night he cried.

Lewis Gordon (12)

Listen To Me

Listen to me, where do we go from here?
There's something in the atmosphere that's changing our lives forever.
I love you, but you keep turning me away,
And now I'm taking that lonely road

Please take me back today, for I'm lost without you,
Please let me stay and we'll work it out together.

Can't you realise that my love yearns for your touch?
To take me out of the darkness and into the light.
Into sunshine, into the sky,
Where I float above the clear blue on the wings of love
And with your arms around me to never let me go.

Please take me back today, for I'm lost without you,
Please let me stay and we'll work it out together.
Together.
I love you.

Alexandra Wharton (16)

Untitled

Lennon wrote lyrics, McCartney too
I hear what you say and
I know what you do
You think I'm a bit lost in the head
Well, let me tell you something,
You ain't seen nothing yet

I'm just a person
A human and a person
I am the shabby
The world is the chic

I am a person
A human and a person
And guess what?
I'm certainly unique.

Eleanor Holloway-Pratt (14)

Enlightened

She did what she had always done
So had what she had always had
Her world was good which she knew
One day she saw a shooting star
It was the single most beautiful thing
Seconds later her world was restored
Yet now she only saw darkness
Days passed and nothing changed
Grief washed over her like the ocean
The darkness consuming her
She knew the star could never love her like this
So she decided to change
She aspired to inspire
So became all she had ever dreamed of
The star returned and was drawn to her light
Together they showed the world they could shine.

Holly Poyner (15)

Not Over You

The way your smile
Took me by surprise
We got talking
Everything we had came back to life
I was happy
And it was my turn to talk
But words wouldn't leave my mouth
I'd lost the battle that I'd fought

Chorus
Cos then you walked away
Left me standing there once again
I saw you reappear
Next to the girl who put the sparkle in your eyes
That's when I realised –
I'm still not over you.

Erin Clague (15)

Unloved

Home after home, carer after carer
If my parents loved me, would life be fairer?
Put up for adoption, I went back down
Won't show no emotion, I won't even frown
Facing the world as one little kid
I try to forget the things that you did
Will never forget when you walked out the door
But I'm older now, you can't hurt me no more
A father should care, a father should love
But instead of a hug you decide to shove
Instead of gentle words you wanted to shout
No warm hugs, just wanted to clout
Shame on you, you will go to Hell
Here I am with a story to tell
Your actions were wrong, they weren't very fair
I'm past even thinkin', I don't even care.

Aishling Collins (17)

Someone Like You

I wanted you to come home today,
But I guess that feeling's got to go away,
I wanted you to hold me close to you,
But I never, ever wanted you to leave,
But I never, ever felt this way before.

I need you to love me,
For you to hold my dreams,
I need someone like you,
To lift my spirit up in the air.

Oh ...
To lift my spirit up in the air,
Oh ...
Someone like you in my heart,
Mmmm ...

Nadia Louise Grassom (17)

Valentine

No girl can match her, no girl can catch her,
She far in the distance, no one can have her, but me,
She my girl, I love every single feature,
My mind's in a twist, every time I see her,
Meet her, trust, I ain't never gonna cheat or deceive her,
I feel her and I wanna treat her,
To diamonds and pearls but she just want me,
I know that I'm young, but I think that I need her,
I believe her, twenty-four seven,
When her lips meet mine, I feel I'm in Heaven,
I get lost in her crystal clear eyes of blue,
Perfect face and body, she just right my boo,
She feel the same for me and I know it,
She know how to show it and I don't wanna throw it away,
It be twelve at night, but like the sun, she shine,
They no girl like mine, that's why she my Valentine.

Adam Lynch (17)

Vivid Flower

Something unexplainable, beautiful, frightening,
Like seeing the thunder, like hearing the lightning,
My future approaching, a tumultuous pace,
But I'm not scared of the danger I face.
Now on the wind comes a beautiful thing,
My vision blurs, and my ears ring,
The tempest draws nearer, closer every hour,
And I start to bloom; a vivid flower.
A howling wind, the storm is soon to arrive,
Now I'm filled with joy as I fight to survive.
The tempest rages, tries to tear me apart,
And I feel ecstatic at the beat of my heart.
The sky is clear, there are no clouds,
They haven't gone but I'm above them now,
I'm hanging suspended, so high in the air,
I know it could kill me and I know I don't care.

Eloise Heath (13)

Being Un-Scene

I'm moving through the crowd
Feeling totally invisible
Trying to find myself
Finding it really hard
Want to curl up and hide
I walk through a bunch of teens
They look me up and down
Mutter something
I miss what they mean
It makes me feel small and
Insignificant
Like I don't belong at all
I need to run
To get away
To find myself
Somehow, some way.

Bethan Pitt (14)

Come And Hold Me Tight

In the darkest night,
Come and hold me tight,
In my fantasy,
You're haunting me.
When I scream out your name,
Do you feel my pain?
Cos tonight my guardian angel,
You need to come and hold me tight.
You're not alone,
I wish I were like you,
Do you wait for me again?
Do you remember me?
As it hurts as I scream,
Come hold me tight,
Never let me go,
In this endless night.

Emily Humphreys (14)

Day By Day

Sit awake, alone
Not a sound, but the quake of your heart
I wonder helplessly, when's the time gonna come?
Just the tick of the clock and the morning sun

I need you, more than anything, now I'm gonna win
Though it's a quick sensation, it goes through me so slow,
And the rain fell down as the sun rose up,
And the fire it burned as my heart just throbbed
But it's the breath you take that keeps me goin'
Day by day

I walk the street, counting cracks in the pavement
Singing songs, of the movie that we saw
Remember that poem we wrote
About the girl in the bright pink coat
As she sang, down the lane, under the shining stars?

Lucy Dinsdale (13)

Loves Way

I don't want to interfere,
you can love her if you want to,
'cause you were mine,
I wanted that to stay the same,
but it didn't,
'cause you loved her,
she loved you,
now that's all I can say,
nothing stayed the same,
ohhh!
the same,
do, do, da, da, do,
'cause nothing stayed the same,
now that's loves way,
'cause everything's loves way.

Lauren Willoughby (11)

324

Sweetest Hello

I was walking down the street ... oh oh oh hoo.
Listening to the song birds humming a sweet tune.
I didn't know where I was going, la la la la.
But I was just swaying where the wind blew me.
I could smell the sweetest chocolate fudge
dance around my taste buds,
round and round, hmm, yer.
Everything was so sweet to me, oh, so sweet.
There wasn't a cloud in the sky,
so I couldn't really say goodbye.
Because all I had to say was the sweetest hello.
Just remember the sweetest hello.
Oh hoo hoo ho.
The simple phrase with a whole lot of feeling, yer, yer.
It can make you feel like the world is in your grasp ... today.
So just remember, the sweetest helloooo.

Abby Holmes (11)

Young Writers Information

We hope you have enjoyed reading this
book - and that you will continue to enjoy it
in the coming years.

If you like reading and writing poetry drop us
a line, or give us a call, and we'll send you a
free information pack.

Alternatively if you would like to order further
copies of this book or any of our other titles, then
please give us a call or log onto our website at
www.youngwriters.co.uk

Young Writers Information
Remus House
Coltsfoot Drive
Peterborough
PE2 9JX
(01733) 890066